WIRED FOR SUCCESS

WIRED FOR SUCCESS

USING NLP TO ACTIVATE YOUR BRAIN FOR MAXIMUM ACHIEVEMENT

WENDY JAGO

JEREMY P. TARCHER/PENGUIN

a member of Penguin Group (USA) Inc.

New York

JEREMY P. TARCHER/PENGUIN
Published by the Penguin Group
Penguin Group (USA) Inc., 375 Hudson Street, New York, New York 10014, USA • Penguin Group
(Canada), 90 Eglinton Avenue East, Suite 700, Toronto, Ontario M4P 2Y3, Canada (a division of
Pearson Penguin Canada Inc.) • Penguin Books Ltd, 80 Strand, London WC2R 0RL, England •
Penguin Ireland, 25 St Stephen's Green, Dublin 2, Ireland (a division of Penguin Books Ltd) • Penguin
Group (Australia), 250 Camberwell Road, Camberwell, Victoria 3124, Australia (a division of Pearson
Australia Group Pty Ltd) • Penguin Books India Pvt Ltd, 11 Community Centre, Panchsheel Park,
New Delhi–110 017, India • Penguin Group (NZ), 67 Apollo Drive, Rosedale, North Shore 0632,
New Zealand (a division of Pearson New Zealand Ltd) • Penguin Books (South Africa) (Pty) Ltd,
24 Sturdee Avenue, Rosebank, Johannesburg 2196, South Africa ·

Penguin Books Ltd, Registered Offices: 80 Strand, London WC2R 0RL, England

First published in the United Kingdom by Piatkus in 2010
First American edition published by Tarcher/Penguin in 2012
Copyright © 2010 by Wendy Jago

Most Tarcher/Penguin books are available at special quantity discounts for bulk purchase for sales
promotions, premiums, fund-raising, and educational needs. Special books or book excerpts also can
be created to fit specific needs. For details, write Penguin Group (USA) Inc. Special Markets,
375 Hudson Street, New York, NY 10014.

ISBN 978-0-399-16042-4

Printed in the United States of America
1   3   5   7   9   10   8   6   4   2

Book design by Paul Saunders

While the author has made every effort to provide accurate telephone numbers, Internet
addresses, and other contact information at the time of publication, neither the publisher
nor the author assumes any responsibility for errors, or for changes that occur after
publication. Further, the publisher does not have any control over and does not
assume any responsibility for author or third-party websites or their content.

In loving memory of Alice Jago, 1913–2009

Acknowledgments

Many people contributed to what has become my personal "NLP account," including those who, like my parents and many of my teachers at school and university, truly helped exercise my thinking about thinking long before NLP itself was formulated.

My NLP roots were in the practice of hypnosis and psychotherapy, and perhaps my biggest debt of all is to the trainer who first introduced me to the early writings of Bandler and Grinder. Sadly, I cannot now recover his name, but if you are out there and read this, I cannot thank you enough.

I have been very fortunate in my NLP teachers, colleagues and coaches, each of whom in different ways helped me feel part of the NLP spirit and the continuing NLP community of inquirers and explorers. I take responsibility for any omissions and extravagances in the true NLP spirit of "it was the best I could do at the time."

Specifically, I owe a huge thank you to Jan Pye, Su Reid and my husband, Leo, who each patiently and supportively read successive drafts of the manuscript and left it better than when they started.

I value greatly the confidence shown in me by Gill Bailey, who commissioned this book, the editorial strengths—both large- and small-chunk!—of Claudia Dyer and Jan Cutler, and the design skills of Paul Saunders, who has polished and splendidly set most of my books and in so doing rendered them beautiful as well as functional.

What brings a message to life is the story it tells. Some of my coaching clients have generously agreed to let their stories be told and their words quoted, and to them I am immensely grateful. Others (both individual and organizational) prefer to remain unidentified, and their stories have been altered or disguised but honored nonetheless.

To all of you, my warmest thanks. This book would not have been possible without you.

Contents

Introduction

We live at a time when everything is changing faster than ever before in human history. Children are growing up taking computers, air travel, the Internet and payment by plastic for granted. News can travel the globe in seconds. This is a very different, and difficult, world in which to navigate, and adaptability is the key to managing it.

You don't need wealth, status or a degree to develop your skill in using the information this book contains, because it's all to do with using your brain—using it more fully and better than you have in the past. The ability to think flexibly in times of rapid social, personal and economic change is a skill you can develop, one that helps you respond inventively and appropriately in a changing and challenging world. Curiously enough, it's often at times of challenge that new opportunities occur. For both of these, our brain is our best asset.

This is a book about building your brain's capacity and effectiveness through targeted exercise. It doesn't have to be an effort. It doesn't need to leave you exhausted or sore, and it doesn't require you to get cold, wet or out of breath. It can be exciting, and I promise you that it can also be fun!

We feel familiar with our brains, just as we do with our bodies. We think we know pretty well what they are capable of, and what they're not. Actually, we underestimate ourselves, and this is the starting point for this book. Think about bodybuilding. If you have never exercised or played sports regularly, there may be times when you have envied those who do: it would be good to be as toned, as supple, as quick and as flexible as they are. If you have been consistently active, your experience will remind you that this is how you became fitter: consistency also made you more skillful—and able to do even more. Exercise and know-how add up to something more than mere fitness—a level of ability greater than you believed yourself capable of.

Although everyone knows that they can acquire more knowledge (as in information), most people—if they think at all about the actual way their brain works—assume that it's somehow in-built and unchangeable. This is not the case, as the early developers of the discipline now known as NLP (neurolinguistic programming) discovered.

SO WHAT IS NLP?

NLP has sometimes been called "the brain-user's manual" because it explains the components of thinking and how we use them in daily life. Once you have discovered a pattern of use that already works for you, you can reuse it in the future or teach it to someone else. When you watch someone who is particularly skilled in what they do, whether it's practical or intellectual, interpersonal or solitary, domestic or on the world's stage, you can admire their achievement—but without a "manual" you can't emulate it. With detailed descriptions and guidelines for use, however, you can make a start. With practice, you may even become excellent! NLP offers you those descriptions and guidelines.

In the 1970s the American cofounders of NLP, John Grinder and Richard Bandler, gathered a group of brilliant young people around them, working together to understand just how people go about thinking and communicating. Grinder and Bandler's background was in cybernetics and psychology, and their aim was to make "the magical skills of potent psychotherapists available to other practitioners in a learnable and explicit form" (from their book *The Structure of Magic* II, p. 3). Both they and other members of the initial group of investigators have continued developing NLP's understanding and training potential through research, writing and teaching. Among the most outstanding are Robert Dilts, Leslie Cameron-Bandler and Steve and Connirae Andreas (see Further Reading).

The original group sought out the "deep structures" of communication, performing their investigations much as a mechanic might seek to understand a highly complex machine in the total absence of diagrams or written instructions: they observed in great detail, asked searching questions about purposes and effects, and tried to establish underlying principles. (In NLP this process is called "modeling"—the subject of Chapter 13.) Where most forms of psychology and sociology offer us theories—which are inherently unprovable—NLP offers descriptions that can be tested and verified by real-life experience every day.

The work they began in the 1970s grew into neurolinguistic programming (NLP). The therapists who were the subject of the original studies had differing backgrounds and used apparently different techniques; yet all of them helped their clients to change and grow powerfully. The investigators began to realize that although their subjects had different explanations for what they were doing, they were in fact acting and thinking alike. So they searched for the basic structures underlying the skills they were studying, and then endeavored to explain and teach them to others.

UNDERSTANDING THE "HOW?"

How? is the characteristic question in NLP. In fact, the majority of the most useful questions in life begin with this word because it directs attention to processes, steps, skills and sequences—all things that can be discovered, demonstrated, shared, learned and improved upon. "How?" lays bare the structure of the best that we are aiming at, and helps us deconstruct the worst that we would rather avoid. This is why "How?" is the characteristic NLP question.

Nowadays NLP enables practitioners in many fields to become even better at whatever they do, whether they are educators and trainers, sportsmen and women, marketeers, managers in business, health professionals, negotiators or creative and performing artists. All make use of NLP skills— as do thousands, and perhaps by now even millions, of people in their private lives.

GROWING YOUR BRAIN

Exercising your brain really does help build it! Brain scans of London black-cab drivers show that the part of their brains that deals with memory is actually larger and more highly developed than those of non-black-cab drivers. Why? Because if you want to be a black-cab driver, you have to acquire The Knowledge: a comprehensive encyclopedia of London topology—every street and alley, monument and major institution, every one-way street and rat run—committed to memory.

By comparison, the mind-building you can do through reading this book is less strenuous, but in an important way it's even more comprehensive. That's because you're not just memorizing: instead you're learning to master the way your mind filters and stores information and to coach yourself through regular exercises to achieve a whole new level of mental fitness and flexibility.

A USEFUL TOOL FOR EVERYONE

In all my years of working with hundreds of people as a therapist, trainer, coach and writer, I have found the NLP "manual" the most useful way of understanding the functioning of the human brain, and the NLP "toolbox" of pattern-based skills the one that I most often reach into. I have the confidence that it will help me work with my clients—and with myself.

My clients have included housewives and businesspeople, adults and children, people with traumas in their pasts, problems in their present and dreams for their future. We have worked together on personal issues, career choices and possibilities, relationship management at work and home, and on challenges to mental and physical well-being. We have often been aware that mind and body are not separate but deeply interconnected, and that the "presenting problem" is not always the one we need to work on.

INTRODUCING THE META-PROGRAMS

NLP offers us an extensive body of information about the workings of our brains, and it gives us many useful tools for change and development. In this book I concentrate on just one set of mental patterns, but one that, despite its importance and usefulness, has not yet been explained for everyday non-professional readers. It's a pattern known in NLP as meta-programming.

At the core of mental fitness is the ability to organize and make sense of the huge mass of information that comes at you both from the external world and from the workings of your own memory, imagination and learning. People who are excellent thinkers are also expert sorters and brilliant managers of information. We all have the same essential mental filtering mechanisms for doing this, although we use them differently. NLP calls these meta-programs, and this book shows you how to use them with more awareness and more flexibility. Different kinds of information require different filters, and so there are a number of different meta-programs. In this book, I will introduce the most important ones, and show you how to recognize your own preferences and those of people around you.

HOW CAN THIS BOOK HELP YOU?

Understanding how the meta-programs can be used in an everyday setting can benefit everyone, even children. It can help partners, parents and children all become more understanding of their families and better at creating harmony; it can help people navigate the stresses of their social lives and the politics of the workplace. Understanding meta-programs helps you "read" other people, so that you can understand the way they approach and deal with situations. This is particularly invaluable in the workplace or where you are working with teams of people.

HOW TO USE THIS BOOK

In *Wired for Success* you will find:

1. An explanation of how meta-programs work.

2. An understanding of how you and others map the world through your meta-programs, and the effects this has at home and at work.

3. Ways to help you start exploring what happens if you vary how you do things now. What new outcomes might be possible? Using your filters differently will produce different results; using them with understanding and flair can produce results that can be richly and productively different for you and for those around you.

4. Ways to coach yourself—how to be an observer of yourself and to use that perspective to have internal conversations that create fuller possibilities for action.

The book is divided into two parts:

Part One explains and introduces the meta-programs (Chapter 2) and includes brain-building exercises to increase your flexibility in using them. The meta-program chapters that follow can be read in any order. The final chapter of the part introduces the technique of modeling, which started NLP off, and which you can use to help you learn and influence others through example.

Part Two helps you apply all you have discovered in Part One to the real, everyday world of home and work, focusing on some common situations and challenges we all face.

HOW YOUR SKILLS CAN SPREAD

In attempting to answer these questions we help ourselves and others become more flexible and potentially more adaptable.

If you are reading this book with the aim of improving your effectiveness at work, you are likely to discover that things also start going better at home. If you are reading it to help you with your partnering or parenting skills, don't be surprised if your influence and success at work also increase. Don't be surprised, either, if people around you start picking up on the changed you and modeling your behavior.

> 66 It is not the strongest of the species that survives, not the most intelligent that survives. It is the one that is the most adaptable to change. 99
>
> Attributed to CHARLES DARWIN

NLP shows us how to use our minds in the best way possible to help us understand each other, live happily, reduce our stress and work effectively. It's a fascinating voyage of discovery and one that I hope you will enjoy as you begin to benefit from a new and different relationship with yourself and others.

·

PART ONE

HOW YOUR MIND SHAPES UP

This part introduces you to the meta-programs and how they work. Its aim is to help you understand yourself and others more clearly. When you understand your own habitual thinking patterns you can work out how these help or hinder you in your everyday life at work and at home. Learning to become more aware of these processes means you can do more of what works and less of what doesn't.

DOING THINGS DIFFERENTLY

We often wonder why other people do certain things the way they do or why they don't do other things in the way we think might be the most logical or effective. By understanding meta-programs you will be able to recognize how other people operate. You will be able to imaginatively step into their shoes so that you can better understand where they are coming from.

Because these differences between ourselves and others are the result of the way we each do our thinking, to understand about them we need also to appreciate the values and judgments behind them. To do this we need to build mental muscle, and we can do this through the exercises contained in each Part One chapter. Chapter 1 explains why you might want to make this commitment to yourself and what makes it worth doing. This kind of exercise can actually be easy and fun to do.

Chapter 2 explains what meta-programs are, and this is followed by a chapter on each of nine key types, which can be read in any order.

WE ARE A SUM OF OUR PARTS

In real life, each of us has a number of meta-programs "running" simultaneously, which naturally connect with, and interact with, each other. Chapter 12 helps you work with these "stacks" or bundles of meta-programs in managing yourself and your relationships at work and at home.

Chapter 13 explains how you can use the NLP tool of modeling to discover and use all kinds of "best practice" and to set a subtle and effective example to others.

Part Two is designed to help you use what you have learned here in everyday situations.

CHAPTER **1**

Why Challenge Yourself?

Have you ever felt that it was too much trouble to change something—particularly yourself? In the Introduction I mentioned the brain-building exercises: when you read it, did you think, *I'm not an exercise person*? Would you feel differently if you knew that by challenging yourself you would do more than just begin to fix some things that aren't going that well? You would acquire more skill and become more effective in your relationships with others, feel more confident *and* discover that there is more to you, and in you, than you had thought possible.

These are some of the benefits you can get from engaging with yourself—engaging in the respectful, inquiring, challenging and supporting way that a coach would: with the added satisfaction of knowing that you have done it all yourself.

One day when my daughter was little, she and I had an argument. We both got frustrated, and I became just as adamant (and "childlike") as she. My husband eventually took me aside and said that I should back down. "Why?" I protested. "I'm no more in the wrong than she is." "Because you are the one with more options" was the reply.

YOU *CAN* CHANGE YOURSELF

What my husband said was hard to take at the time; but it was a good lesson. The word "options" was the key: it reminded me that I was stuck only for as long as I chose to go on behaving the same way. I remembered, when I needed it most, that although I can't change others directly, I can always challenge and change myself. On that day, the issue wasn't just about retreating from a lose–lose battle to demonstrate who was really in the right: it was about my need to be in the right—at the expense of someone else. It was about being confident enough to say, "I'm sorry," and to take on board what I had to do differently in the future. It wasn't easy, but even when change is effortful it can also be freeing and stimulating. It can even be exciting, like cracking the shell of an old behavior or an old way of thinking and allowing something freer and more powerful to emerge.

How much can we really change?

Challenge and change that involve growth usually seem attractive, but when we confront the possibility of tackling our difficulties or limitations we can initially feel defensive and inadequate. These are the times when we would rather not take ourselves on: it may seem like a lot of effort, and maybe we aren't sure whether we can make a difference anyway.

Personality is often taken for granted, as if it were fixed, and this feeds into the assumption that it's difficult—if not impossible—to make fundamental changes. People who have completed a personality profile (usually at work) sometimes feel their "results" have somehow slotted them into a pigeon-

hole. As one of my clients said, the danger of any categoriz-
ation is that "I walk away thinking it is telling me 'I am' rather
than what I could be. When I think about all of our face-to-
face conversations, that's not how it is: I always walk away
from them thinking about doors having opened and new
links formulated."

The sum of your meta-program preferences is not your
personality. Indeed, it's hard—and perhaps not all that
helpful—to define what "personality" is. Your meta-program
preferences add up to a set of mental habits for making sense
of information—and habits can be changed. Changing the
mental strategies that have become habitual is less about how
we are and more about how we think and what we do. Once
we realize this it can remove any sense of threat and open up
a surprising amount of space and opportunity.

There's so much scope within the meta-program options
for experimenting, stretching and growing. Understanding our habitual "default" position is only a start. If we
are willing to challenge ourselves by experimenting with
other ways of sorting and filtering, then exploring along
each meta-program's range of possibilities can open doors to
new understandings and new behaviors, and allow us to
make creative links within ourselves and to other people.
If we are willing to stretch a little by trying something a bit
different, we can build our mental strength and at the same
time increase our mental agility.

POWER FROM SELF-COACHING

I want to invite you to begin coaching yourself toward
greater meta-program flexibility. Self-coaching offers you powerful strategies, not just for surviving in times of pressure, stress
and challenge but also for thriving. The strategies start helping
you as soon as you begin to view yourself from outside and to

ask yourself questions. Once you do, you become your own investigator, explorer, tutor and supporter. You will be working in one of the most enabling partnerships possible: the partnership you can have with yourself!

A good place to start is with two core assumptions of all coaching. First, that you already have all the resources you need to manage yourself and your life. And second, that there are no inherently wrong ways for doing things, only ones that don't work as well as others.

Starting now

Your starting point is what you currently think, feel and do; your benchmark for development is how much more you might be capable of. Your achievement is how far you manage to narrow the gap. You are the one who sets your targets; you are the one who sets the pace; you are the one who monitors the feedback you get from others and from your own gut feelings and thoughtful reflections.

Coaching assumes you can also become more self-aware. This forms the essential baseline for making any changes in how you manage yourself and your interaction with others. The information you need is there inside you, but many people have learned to ignore their gut feelings and the messages of their stressed or weary bodies, often for the most conscientious or self-effacing of motives. But starting with you doesn't mean you are "selfish." In fact, coaching is based on cultivating your self-awareness, learning to recognize your needs, wants, energy levels, preferences and dislikes, so that you can learn how and when you need to make them a priority. Overriding them, however noble the reason, just means that you are blocking out information that may be critical.

BECOMING EVEN BETTER

Let's not fall into the common trap of assuming that change is only about fixing things. Your reason for not challenging yourself could be that you are comfortable, and perhaps even proud, being the way you are. So, why change anything? Because you could be even better!

Knowing more about your mental strengths allows you to use them more reliably, and to adapt them to new or different situations.

Working with yourself allows you to make informed choices instead of being controlled (and limited) by your habitual default responses. It takes you into your stretch zone.

> **Stretch zone** An area of activity or thought that involves you in a more challenging way than your comfort zone but less than your panic zone. The stretch zone is where growth and learning take place. If you are in your comfort zone, you are not prompted to develop and grow, and when you are in your panic zone these are not possible.

WHAT'S SPECIAL ABOUT SELF-COACHING?

Self-coaching works by developing a more enabling kind of relationship with yourself, by understanding your strengths and identifying any weaknesses or limitations you may have. It leads to good-quality conversations with yourself, to help you discover that you might be able to go beyond what is simply good enough to becoming outstanding. The aim isn't to delete the parts of yourself that you don't like or that cause problems for you: rather, it's about learning to recognize, manage and sometimes take the pressure off them. It isn't about easy self-acceptance, either, although it can certainly help you to be more generous to yourself.

Creating your special coaching space

It helps to set time aside when you can have conversations with yourself. This could be a regular time each day, perhaps when commuting on public transport, where it's relatively easy to close your eyes or stare into space. Or you could use your time while you are in the shower or when going for a run. Alternatively, you may prefer to "seize the moment" for your self-coaching conversations, such as times when you are waiting in a supermarket line, doing the dishes, and so on. You can choose to work in a specific physical space, or you might like to think of these reflective, inquiring times as happening in your own mental coaching space, wherever you physically happen to be.

As you begin to discover your habitual, "default" position on the different meta-programs, you will be noticing what happens *and* how it happens. The brain-building exercises attached to each meta-program have been designed to help you reach out toward the opposite way of thinking, thus increasing the options you have available.

MAKING A START

Challenging yourself is both demanding and enabling. Your baseline for working with yourself in this way is one of respectful inquiry and playful experiment. You do not need to learn a whole body of unfamiliar information. What you are doing is giving labels to something that you have been experiencing ever since you were a small child and that you encounter every day in every context of your life. At your own pace you can become more aware and more flexible in what you do already.

Challenging yourself starts most easily with what comes most easily, which might be just one set of meta-program contrasts that interests, amuses or frustrates you. It doesn't even have to take much time. It's not like learning to speak a language or drive a car—you can start anywhere and there's no sequence you have to follow.

I hope that as you read this book you'll find it shows you new ways to make that voyage of discovery even more rewarding and enjoyable. Now read Chapter 2 to understand all about meta-programming.

CHAPTER **2**

How We Filter Information

In order to get around in the physical world, we need guidance: we need some kind of map. A map is an abstraction from reality, and it is also the result of someone's investigation, thought and decision-making. It is not the "reality" it represents. In the same way that there are different kinds of maps—some that represent physical features and others that represent abstract data—we also work with our own mental maps, not of the physical landscape but of our own mental landscape. These maps simplify and select from billions of pieces of information available to us to help us navigate through all aspects of our lives.

WHAT THE MAPS MEAN TO US

Everyone's mind makes its own idiosyncratic maps, which it then treats as a navigable "reality." The more abstract the concepts—for example, human relationships, environmental issues, economic strategies, financial structures, the meaning of historical events—or the more personally vital the issues are to us, the more idiosyncratic the mental "maps" tend to be. In only a few respects do they reflect any externally demonstrable "reality." Alfred Korzybski, the founder of the theory of general semantics, said that "the map is not the territory." We tend to act "as if" our mental maps were reliable guides; but whereas a geographical map's assumptions about landscape should turn out to be more or less factually accurate when you attempt to use it, the assumptions your mind makes will actually *shape* the personal territory you are journeying in.

Your map: my map

Assumptions made by people, organizations and nations based on "maps" about issues, such as gender, nationhood, government, profit and profitability, for example, have created huge problems, because several apparently viable maps of the territory were simultaneously active. If your "highway" is my "ravine," and we both act according to our private maps, we are likely to misunderstand each other.

Mapping issues can cause trouble within individuals, not just between them. We can't function without maps, but we need to understand them. First, we need to recognize that they are not the same thing as the territory and, second, that we are navigating by maps that we have made up ourselves because of our assumptions, values and attitudes, and we can therefore limit our effectiveness or even cause ourselves actual difficulties.

The way our filters work

If you were making a map of a physical landscape, you would be making use of specific filters. You would choose to indicate that one type of building (for example, a telephone booth) is different from others (it is not a house) and to connect other features (for example, the height of places above sea level) because of their similarities. In other words, how you filter information determines what ends up on your map of "reality."

THE META-PROGRAM FILTERING MECHANISMS

In order to avoid information overload we use our own system for filtering and making sense of it—a set of mental programs, each providing a kind of template that allows certain kinds of information through while blocking out others.

If you have ever been part of a discussion that was being tape-recorded, and then you later listened to the tape, you will probably have been struck by how many extraneous and unrelated sounds you had to filter out as you tried to hear the discussion that seemed audible enough at the time. The tape records the discussion; but it also records the sounds of people coughing, or pushing their chairs back, shifting their weight or shuffling papers, as well as traffic noises from outside, sounds elsewhere in the building, telephones in the distance and so on. However, you simply didn't hear these noises at the time because you were filtering. You were sorting out what you needed to hear. You may also have been filtering in another way: you were likely to be hearing what you had pre-decided was important for you. You may have noticed when someone agreed with your opinion, or disagreed with it. You might have gotten irritated when someone tried to take the discussion off on an irrelevant tack; although, of course, it didn't seem irrelevant to them! You heard what you were interested in. Interpretation, and even memory, is also affected by filtering processes.

How our filters work

When we enter into a situation we already have our mental filters and selective templates (or meta-programs) operating, which means that only rarely do we gather raw data as opposed to pre-selected information. The mental sorting templates and filters we use every day are habitual and often quite unconscious. NLP calls them "meta-programs" because they work in high-level (meta) ways to organize a great deal of material at a lower level, and because they are habitual (programmed-in) to us as individuals. They work rather like the operating systems that manage your computer. They are not what you see on-screen, but they are essential to making the computer work. That's how fundamental, and how essential, your meta-programs are within your brain.

> **Meta-programs** are mental structures that operate at a high level of generality to organize a mass of more specific information. They have the effect of acting as templates or filters that let through certain kinds of information while blocking others.

Each meta-program helps us deal with just one specific kind of information. Part One explains the most significant meta-programs, how they work and what kind of information they manage. You will learn that the way you use them can both limit and enable you.

Are you an overview or a detail person?

Each meta-program template provides for a range of possibilities between two extremes rather like a dimmer control that can slide along a range of possible settings and stop at any position between bright and dim or hot and cold.

On any one meta-program, most people naturally tend to operate nearer one extreme of possibility or the other. Everyone will have their own unconsciously preferred and habitual "default setting." One person prefers big concepts (large chunks) while another is drawn into the detail (small chunks). One person, when trying to fix something broken, naturally looks to the user's manual for instructions: this is a "procedural" approach. Another person is quite happy to tinker and play around with the bits until they find a way to fix it: this is an "inventive" way of going about it.

Once you know your natural default setting on a particular meta-program, you can work out in which circumstances it is useful or limiting to you. You can also begin to imagine what it might be like if you took a different position, and what advantages and disadvantages this might have. In other words, knowledge brings with it the possibility of more choices and greater enjoyment or effectiveness in your life. If you are a big-concepts/principles (large-chunk) person, you may get impatient with a detail (small-chunk) member of your family or team. Knowing how you go about it, making the effort to appreciate just how someone different may think, and learning to respect their way as equally valid in itself, allows you to work alongside them with less stress and to discover where your different approaches can each have something useful to contribute.

Moving away from our default settings

Knowing your default settings and learning how to recognize those of others opens up the prospect of better map-making. But we don't have to be content with the places our default settings take us to, and we certainly don't have to remain limited by them. Filtering options can be modified. Recipes can be varied. Mental muscles can be made more supple and strengthened. That's where the brain-building exercises at the end of each meta-program chapter come in. Practicing them can be exciting, enlightening, strenuous, inspiring—sometimes all of these together! By exercising your brain in unfamiliar ways, you will help it to create new links—literally building new filaments (dendrites) that reach out from one cell to another. By asking your brain to explore avenues that are unfamiliar to it, you create new neural pathways. As you stretch your mental muscles, you will build the capacity of your brain.

CHAPTER **3**

How Big Is Your Bite?

How much information can you handle at once? Some people find that information makes more sense if they start with an overview or bigger picture. Others prefer starting from the detail. At the extremes, some people find detail difficult to work with and others are happiest working with nothing else! In NLP these approaches are referred to as "large-chunk" and "small-chunk."

LARGE vs. SMALL CHUNKS

I once traveled in the cockpit of an aircraft and, looking out from 30,000 feet, was able to see the curvature of the earth for the first time. "I never tire of looking at that," said my friend the pilot. On that same flight I witnessed at first hand the opposite approach—the checking and rechecking of detail fundamental to the performance and safety of the flight. Fuel, distance to point of no return, height and air speed were all calculated and recalculated at set intervals by the co-pilot as well as appearing on the aircraft's instrumentation. Every so often we were transferred from one control tower to another, continuously monitored all the way from the ground as well as in the air. As a passenger, I felt reassured and safe, and I was also made aware of the contrast between the earth-wide span of one perspective on our progress and the minute, close-up way of managing it that lay behind the calculations and safety checks. The detailed checks were essential for the overall direction and safety of the journey. On the other hand, the journey's destination was what gave the detail its purpose and meaning.

I was getting a real demonstration of two ways of managing the same information: each view virtually ignored the other, although ultimately, of course, these contrasting approaches filtered the available information in ways that between them gave an understanding that was richer and more comprehensive just because it was more complex.

Why both matter

Between them, large-chunk and small-chunk sorting control the way we manage, contextualize and specify information. They also often complement each other. Detail acquires significance through being a part of the bigger picture, whereas the bigger picture is made live and meaningful by the detail it contains. For some things in life, we need to take a broad view: for others, we need to get in really close. Let's look at how each works.

BEING A LARGE-CHUNK PROCESSOR

Large-chunk processors feel most at home when they can get a sense of how things are overall or in the round. They prefer large categories or classes of information, seeking to place detail within them. They seek out general, often abstract, labels and concepts that indicate significance, intention, purpose and achievement. For them, detail is only meaningful when it can be subsumed into one of these.

Advantages

If you're a large-chunk processor, you will naturally take an overview of the situation, which can be helpful for planning, evaluating and managing. You are likely to be good at brainstorming or visioning (creating big pictures). Large-chunk processors are also often inventive (see Chapter 4). You are good at contextualizing and seeing where things fit in—or where they don't.

Disadvantages

The disadvantage of large-chunk processing may be that it is simply too broad a brush to work with in practice. "Blue-sky" ideas may never translate to earth! Once you have had your grand idea, you may be irritated with requests to flesh it out or tidy it up, and feel impatient with others who ask you to supply the details that will help them make it happen. You may also be daunted by large tasks, because even though you naturally "work large" and grasp the idea of the task as a whole, you may find it difficult to plan the specific steps that will get it done. You may also be what is known as "in-time": this means that you very much live in the present and don't naturally tend to relate your experiences in relation to the past or future. (I explain this in detail in Chapter 5.) If you naturally see things in large chunks, you can easily get impatient with yourself and others about the time it takes to get things done.

BEING A SMALL-CHUNK PROCESSOR

Small-chunkers are happiest with detail—indeed, they may be very good at it. You may have an excellent memory, because you have stored each detail of an experience, and this helps preserve it in all its complexity and richness. For this reason, you can readily recall and relive experiences. If you are describing something to someone, either your listener will appreciate the fullness of your account or they may get lost in the detail, because for them it may not seem to relate to an overall "story."

Advantages

If your focus is close-up and your recall good, you are likely to show aptitude with anything requiring precision. You may enjoy managing figures or working with complex processes. You may be good at science and find information technology effortless. Patience will probably be one of your virtues in doing tasks, because you will be content to let each small chunk dictate its own pace. You will approach problems step by step until they are solved. Being a small-chunk processor can often connect with being methodical and thorough—even, perhaps, a perfectionist.

Disadvantages

As a small-chunk processor you may be less good at grasping the bigger picture, or at cueing others in to the story you are telling, or the point you are trying to make, because cueing in requires you to offer your listener a "headline" or "signpost" that tells them where you are going. For you, these aren't needed; but if you're talking to larger-chunk processors these cues may be an essential framework that helps them make sense of what you're trying to tell them. Without a heading, they can only follow you detail by detail, which they may find frustrating or even irritating. In meetings, people may get impatient with you because you haven't gotten to the point: friends and family may sometimes feel you are rambling. You may spend more time than is needed on a task, because you do it in more detail than is required. Co-workers might find you one-paced and inflexible in your way of going about things. As far as they are concerned you plod along, giving every task the same amount of your time and attention regardless of its merits.

WHAT'S YOUR DEFAULT SETTING?

Have you ever been at a work meeting when somehow the focus seemed to disappear? The chances are that a number of people felt so strongly about something that they focused on just that. This probably provoked an equally close-up focus from someone else with a point to make, and pretty soon everyone was floundering in a sea of detail. They had lost sight of the point, the context, the overall frame that would make it meaningful. Both are needed—and this is where your meta-program flexibility comes in, because it helps you adjust and readjust the balance.

Other meetings may suffer from the opposite approach: people get carried away with principles and abstract ideas, while somewhere in the group at least one person is thinking, *How do I start*?

The same thing happens outside of work, of course. Years ago when our daughter was little, and before I had learned about the NLP meta-programs, we had a family ritual of asking each other, "How was your day?" I noticed that both my husband and daughter tended to plunge straight away into the details of what they had done, but this made me impatient, because I wanted to have an impression of what the day had been like for them overall. I wanted them to start off by saying something like: "I had a great day because . . ." or "I had a horrible day because . . ." or "Today was different/ interesting because . . ." I needed a "signpost" that would set what followed in context. The very words "signpost" and "context" now tell me that I naturally prefer large-chunk settings to explain and help me make meaning of the detail that follows.

Spot your natural preference

Human beings have many possible resting places on the continuum between broad and narrow focus, between big picture and close-up. Phrases used in everyday speech will give you some idea of your natural preference, and that of other people.

Large-chunk	Small-chunk
Are you an "overview" person?	Are you more comfortable with detail?
Do you light up at visionary ideas?	Do you like to "home in" on things?
Do you go for "the big picture"?	Do you prefer a "close-up" view?
Are you "broad brush" in the way you describe ideals and goals?	Do you go for a "tight brief"?
Do you like to know how your "piece of the jigsaw" fits in with the rest?	Do you find it hard to see the wood for the trees?

THE BEST OF BOTH WORLDS

When you take a shot through the lens of a camera, the success of the resulting picture will depend on the appropriateness of the image you select, irrespective of whether you are using manual or automatic. Getting the best of both large- and small-chunk sorting is a bit like remembering to use your zoom (either in or out) so that you get the kind of picture that does justice to both you and your subject.

If you have ever tried to take a snapshot of a view, you may well have been disappointed, when you looked later at the picture you took, to find that the image lacks meaning and detail. In life, your eye supplies these by rapid, and often quite unnoticed, alterations of focus. It's because you haven't appreciated that you were making these adjustments yourself in order to get the full picture that you are disappointed later on. On the other hand, if you go really close in to take a shot of a particular object, you may find afterward that it lacks the meaning that context would give it. If you went in really, really close, it might be hard to tell from the photo what size the object is, or even what it is!

In each situation, the important thing is to get the relationship between the bigger concept and the detail right for the situation and for the outcome that's needed.

How knowing your default setting helps

Recognizing your "default setting" is the first step to becoming more effective, because it means you can work with your natural preference while at the same time using the opposite default as a check and balance. Here are some examples from work and home life:

1. If you have a goal that involves other people, you can work from detail (for example, an initial contact about a work

project via e-mail or phone) right through to the large-chunk result (for example, the launch of a new system). Or you can work from the overall goal down to the detail that makes it happen. Let's suppose, for example, that you have been asked to reorganize your department's accounts.

If you are small-chunk	If you are large-chunk
You will probably enjoy the detailed working out of a new system.	You may feel comfortable with the idea of helping to increase efficiency.
Remind yourself that the purpose of the exercise involves larger issues, such as speeding up the backtracking of orders or providing a clearer and quicker access to the bottom line of profitability/loss.	**Remind yourself** that this will only be achieved through making the right changes in the details as well as the principles of the existing systems.

2. Perhaps you are planning a family holiday abroad and want to make the most of your time in a capital city you haven't visited before. You can achieve a good outcome either by working outward from the specific experiences you want to include or inward from your overall vision of the "ideal holiday."

If you are small-chunk	If you are large-chunk
There may be lots of activities and excursions you'd like to include in your schedule.	You're likely to hope for outcomes like "enjoying the history of the place" or "experiencing different customs."

chart continues on next page ➤

If you are small-chunk

Remind yourself that you need to look at how the days' activities will stack up: Will your family get tired, or bored? Will they want some days free of any planning, just to relax and chill out?

If you are large-chunk

Remind yourself that although these may come about by accident, you can also do some more detailed advance planning to make them more likely. Check in advance on what each member of the family would like, and spend time on some detailed investigation about what's available (including excursions you can book, and passes and tickets you can buy before leaving home). Specific strategies like these can ensure your grand hopes do actually turn into realities.

BRAIN-BUILDING EXERCISES

EXERCISE 1 *Zooming in and out*

Ultimately, you are aiming for increased flexibility and ease at zooming between large- and small-chunk processing. The ability to adjust your zoom is an invaluable tool for understanding situations, setting things in context, and assimilating new information into what you already know, as well as planning, strategizing and formulating goals that can actually come to fruition.

One way to develop more flexibility in using different

➤

chunk sizes is to think of them as specialized functions that have different, but essential, contributions to make to your thinking.

Large-chunk labels and small-chunk details together add up to something others can easily follow and more easily share in. Each complements the other.

Let's imagine you want to tell your family an anecdote over supper, or outline a proposal or plan at work. Here is a step-by-step program to help you do it effectively.

1. Ask yourself what the point of the story is. You are looking for the theme, the peg around which your idea hangs, the kernel of what you want to achieve through your plan. Milton's epic poem *Paradise Lost* tells us in its very first words that the poem's subject is

   Of man's first disobedience, and the fruit
   Of that forbidden tree . . .

   It's going to be about Adam and Eve and the consequences of eating the apple in the Garden of Eden. What's your story going to be about?

2. If you find it hard to identify your underlying theme or point immediately, it may be because you naturally think in small chunks. In that case, take a few of the details and ask yourself:

   • What do they have in common?
   • What is this all about?

3. You are looking for a single word, or at most a short phrase that highlights a larger concept which embraces your particular example(s). The titles of long-running

   ➤

television soaps are good examples of how this process works: *Neighbors, Coronation Street, ER*. What's the underlying theme?

4. Once you are clear in your own mind about what you want to communicate, put yourself in the shoes of your listeners. You are going to give them a starting signpost or label. Once this has given them the key idea of your story or plan, what details or examples can you give that will catch their imagination or show them how it works in practice? Use what you already know about the way they think to help you get the right pitch.

If you know that their default position with regard to chunk size is like yours, you will be at home and most effective talking in your own most natural way. If you know their default is different from yours you can either follow up your "heading" with more broad-brush ideas or you can move straight into sharing the detail with them.

EXERCISE 2 *When is enough?*

Both large- and small-chunkers can have problems knowing when they have done enough. The large-chunker may have a sneaking feeling that something is missing from a piece of work, or that someone else may catch them out or think they have been skimping. Past experience may tell them that colleagues sometimes think them slapdash. The small-chunker may have been criticized in the past for taking too long over a project, or of getting lost in an unnecessary amount of detail.

➤

1. The first thing you need to find out (from the person who wants you to do the work, or whoever you are attempting to communicate with) is: What would they consider to be an adequate job? Do they just want you to put forward a few ideas for discussion? Do they want a few comments "off the top of your head" to guide their own thinking? Or do they want something worked through in careful and accurate detail?

2. In other words, in order to know "when is enough" you have to weigh both your estimate of what "enough" means and what your recipient, listener or customer is likely to find adequate. A very simple way to get this right is to ask them beforehand! There is rarely any advantage in guessing. By getting a "recipe for success" in advance, you not only make a satisfactory outcome more likely but you will also exercise and build on your own flexibility through working to different tolerances.

EXERCISE 3 *Skeleton and flesh*

This exercise can help you to analyze written or spoken presentations to extract the meat from them and, on the other hand, it can ensure that when you write or present something you put it together coherently and economically.

1. First you need to analyze someone else's argument. For this you will need a pad and pen. You may find it easier to start by analyzing written material, as you can take as much time as you need. When listening, you are more likely to feel pressured by the need to keep up with the

➤

speaker. As you read, keep asking yourselfs "And the point is?" Every time you identify a phrase or brief statement that seems to make a point, underline it if you're working from print, or jot it down if you are listening. Ignore detail; just go for the major points being made. You are looking for the bones. You will end up with a list of items that seem to have equal value or status, rather like this:

2. When you have finished, look at the points you have jotted down. Are they all of equal weight, or are some of them comments on, or examples of, others? If some are like this, rewrite your list indenting the subsidiary points to show that function. Your list might now look like this:

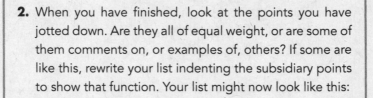

3. Can you find an overall theme or heading? (It might not be the one that the writer originally gave to the document!) If so, put it at the top. Can you think of a concluding, wrapping-up statement? If so, put it at the end.

➤

You now have an outline plan for what you have read:

Title ▬▬▬▬▬▬▬▬▬▬▬▬▬▬▬▬▬

Point 1 ▬▬▬▬▬▬▬▬▬▬▬▬▬▬▬

    Sub-point ▬▬▬▬▬▬▬▬▬▬▬▬

Point 2 ▬▬▬▬▬▬▬▬▬▬▬▬▬▬▬

    Sub-point ▬▬▬▬▬▬▬▬▬▬▬▬

    Sub-point ▬▬▬▬▬▬▬▬▬▬▬▬

Conclusion ▬▬▬▬▬▬▬▬▬▬▬▬▬

4. Now you have the skeleton, and this will help you see the relationship between the skeleton and the "flesh" of analogies, examples, facts and general padding that are attached to it. Do the examples or illustrations fit in? Do they illustrate or help prove the points they're attached to?

With practice, you can get really quick at doing this, and feel confident to use the same strategy for analyzing spoken presentations.

When you want to plan a written or spoken presentation of your own, use the same method: it will help you, regardless of whether you are naturally a small- or a large-chunk person. It will ensure that both your outline and the thread of your argument are clear and that you support them appropriately with detail to engage your target audience.

HOW THEY DO IT

Fiona Davenport, health service manager

❝I am naturally a detail person. In my appraisal it was pointed out that this sometimes means I spend too long on writing and write too much. I used the idea of changing chunk size to plan a report around bullet points, and rationed myself to a couple of sentences for each. My manager said this gave her just the amount of information she needed—and because writing like this took much less time it freed me up for other work I needed to get done. I didn't find it at all easy to change my way of working, but I was very pleased I had made myself do it. In the past, I believed that every report had to be done as thoroughly as possible. Now I've learned that less detail can sometimes make for a better job. I know I can choose how much detail to include according to what's really needed. I'm more confident because I've found I can do an equally good job in several ways, not just one.❞

CHAPTER **4**

How Do You Go About Solving Problems?

A task or problem can be tackled in two contrasting ways: either procedurally or inventively. You can make use of established and orderly procedures, or you can be inventive, seeking new or customized approaches. When I was a teenager first learning to cook, I relied on recipe books and was pleased to get good results. Taking a procedural approach ensured that things mostly didn't go wrong. I even had one recipe book that explained what procedures were involved in creating failures: it had a very useful section with headings like:

If your cake doesn't rise it's because . . .

If your cake rises and then falls it's because . . .

If your cake has a hole in it, it's because . . .

Over the years my way of cooking changed, because experience had prepared me to go beyond what I already knew would work. I had internalized most basic procedures, so I was free to use my imagination more. My cooking gradually became less procedural and more inventive.

BEING PROCEDURAL vs. BEING INVENTIVE

My recipe book enshrined what later became an important and useful NLP axiom. There are "recipes" for failure just as much as there are for success. Some failure recipes are pretty universal: for example, if you disregard the other person's point of view, you cannot predict their responses to what you do or say and you may run into more trouble than you bargained for. Equally, we each have our individual failure recipes: steps and sequences we habitually follow that get us into trouble every time!

THE BENEFITS OF EACH APPROACH

Procedures help us achieve predictable results and maintain quality, but by definition they repeat what has been done before. If we rely on established procedures we are limited by the thinking that underpins them. Inventive approaches can result in exciting new discoveries—or in disasters. Creativity that works out is usually well founded and well prepared. This meta-program governs how you approach problems and tasks. Being flexible on this meta-program doubles your chances of solving problems effectively.

The orderly approach

At one end of the spectrum are people who prefer procedures—especially order, sequence and comprehensiveness. This rests upon an underlying belief that there is a right or best way. This may be linked to another belief, which is that the right or best way has already been established and needs only to be followed with confidence in order to achieve a satisfactory outcome each time. Even if someone is following a pattern they established themselves, they are likely to feel more comfortable with it. If you frequently drive between certain places, for example, you're likely to take the same route almost without thinking. Habit is procedural.

Creating new approaches

At the other end of the spectrum are people who prefer treating each task or problem as unique. Even if what confronts you is not new in itself, you get the most pleasure inventing from scratch, suiting the method to the individual task. An inventive driver might choose to vary their regular commute by taking different routes on different days.

UNDERSTANDING THE TWO VIEWS

This meta-program helps shape how you approach opportunities, choices and crises in your life, because at a deep level it touches on your feelings about risk and security. Individuals don't always take the same approach to everything, though. Depending on what's involved for them at this deep level, the very same person can be clearly procedural at some times or in some areas of their lives while being equally clearly inventive in others.

It's relatively obvious that both extremes are selective: each viewpoint not only goes about things differently but also rests on a cluster of important values and judgments. One approach takes it that procedures are worth following because they are reliable and proven by experience. The other approach rests on the implicit belief that new and different is likely to be better, and that a method individually tailored to the problem will result in a more fitting solution.

From the procedural view, the inventive approach can seem risky or gimmicky. From the inventive standpoint, established ways may seem to make things tidy for tidiness' sake and risk straitjacketing the problem into a pre-existing formula. Both views may actually share the belief that the real world is messy, but whereas one assumes that order can be brought out of chaos, the other assumes that the world can best be dealt with on a customized basis.

Convergent vs. divergent thinking

Procedural thinkers usually bring information together, refining it toward a single solution. This approach is known as "convergent." Inventive thinkers, on the other hand, look outward from what's already been established and seek to broaden the base of their thinking. Their approach is "divergent."

BEING PROCEDURAL

You are more comfortable doing things "by the book." You innately respect the steps and sequences that have been evolved over time to create products, manage complex, tricky or risky situations, and ensure people are safe and that everything that needs to be thought of has been thought of. Organizations and institutions as large as the legal profession or as small as a local playgroup all have more or less formalized procedures for managing what they do. The education system has developed processes to ensure that learning is organized in an orderly and sequenced way, with formal tests and markers at different levels that tell pupils, parents and potential employers what standards the learner has reached. Scientific communities in schools, universities and industry have protocols that ensure safe working and that allow proof and value to be demonstrated, checked and made consistent. Flying aircraft and performing surgery both rest on the careful carrying out of checks and routines.

Procedural people and organizations are not against what is new in a crude or absolute sense. They recognize that there is a place in the procedural world for new developments. They are likely to be evolved as advances or refinements on products and practices that already exist. Given a problem, the procedural person or organization will seek solutions through tightening up or improving established practice.

Advantages

Procedural people are good at carrying out complex tasks because they want to ensure everything gets done correctly, at the right time and in the right order. They are usually responsible and reliable, although they may work more slowly than people with a more cavalier or inventive approach. In work teams, they are essential doers and completers. They check up and help the team avoid errors. They manage libraries and archives, check quality and progress and maintain consistency of standards. They are essential for the reliability and efficiency of all organizations, including families and friendship groups.

Disadvantages

By definition, procedures don't cover things that haven't happened before. And in emergencies or when something occurs out of the blue it's not always possible to consult the relevant rule book! Professions that rely on procedures for effectiveness and safety, such as medicine, finance and the law, tend to have long and elaborate training periods (more procedures!), which require trainees to learn and remember a wealth of key information. Memory is vastly important. When I was working as a hypnotherapist, one of my clients was a policeman who had trouble learning the law he needed for everyday policing. Police work requires that very specific forms of language are used in certain situations: for example, when cautioning suspects and informing them of their rights. My client sought help because memorizing by rote was the one aspect of policing he found virtually impossible to master. Professions that rely on procedures also take care to anticipate things that may go wrong and to train their staff through drills and rehearsals. Large-scale disasters can show up both the strengths and the weaknesses of this approach.

Being procedural often links up with looking at things close up—indeed, it has to, because complex procedures are made up of ordered steps and sequences. So, procedural people may find that less procedural colleagues, friends and family members can get impatient or even exasperated with them at times. In their turn, they can be irritated by people who are not as careful about detail as they are, or who have a more casual attitude toward rules and regulations. They can be so aware of "the rules," both explicit and implicit, that they feel responsible even when they are not. Public situations in which strangers' children are misbehaving, or where it seems another adult is bending the rules, can upset them out of all proportion to the "offense" they are witnessing. Seeing someone jumping a line, for example, or "getting away with" not paying for parking, may make them feel they should intervene personally.

A procedural person won't find it easy to cut corners or do a less than perfect job. And they will find it hard to "hurry up" because for them varying their pace could mean they skimp or leave out something vital. By nature, they will put as much effort into something trivial as into something important, because as far as they are concerned everything needs to be done properly. In coaching procedural people I have sometimes needed to work to destabilize this unconsidered conscientiousness by pointing out that a certain job could actually be done most perfectly if they did skimp or hurry a bit! To devote the same energy and care to something that is done for a short-term impression—or which is not designed to last for long—as you would devote to something that involves safety or that needs to work reliably over a long time is actually less than properly procedural! For a procedural person, getting their head around a paradox such as this can actually be very liberating, because it gets them thinking about the relationship between the "what?" and the "how?" of the task or challenge they are facing. In determining how they should go about something, procedural people can become subtler and more effective by factoring in issues like context, purpose and risk.

BEING INVENTIVE

Inventive people prefer to find their own way of doing things. Given a problem, they will usually ignore or bypass approaches that have been tried before, and look for new, different ways of tackling it. Where procedural people seek to improve what already exists, inventive people are looking for what doesn't exist. Focusing on the problem gets an inventive person "brainstorming" until something quite new emerges as a solution.

> 66 People build something that works. Then circumstances change, and they have to tinker with it to make it continue to work, and they are so busy tinkering that they cannot see that a much better idea would be to build a whole new system to deal with the new circumstances. 99
>
> TERRY PRATCHETT, *Monstrous Regiment*, p. 80

Advantages

Inventive people may become designers, artists or problem-solvers. Their creative approach can make them good consultants in many fields, because they are not trapped by existing ways of thinking and can offer new insights and approaches. They may be able to respond creatively to apparently insoluble problems. They are not afraid of taking risks, and may actively enjoy challenges that others have found difficult or impossible. If you are looking for a new approach, or for a way out or through a stuck situation, an inventive person may be just what you need. Wit, fun and humor all draw on inventiveness, since they rely for effect on the unexpected or the incongruent.

In solving problems, inventive people may put known facts or details together, but it will be in a way that hasn't previously been thought of. Christopher Cockerell, who invented the hovercraft, knew that air under pressure creates a cushion and can, in a confined space, lift considerable weight. His novel idea was that if this air cushion was surrounded by a flexible rubber skirt it could support a moving vehicle over an undulating surface—water—as well as over a stable one: land.

Disadvantages

Wrestling with how to solve the problem is half the fun for inventive people—more enjoyable than actually putting the solution into practice! This can mean that while an inventive person is great at dreaming up new projects or new ways of tackling existing problems, they are likely to find the follow-through stages much less attractive. For this, a procedural person is required. If you are inventive, you may be so excited by what you have dreamed up that you underestimate both its difficulties and its risks.

An extremely inventive person is always going to want to move on to the next thing, which means they are likely to lose interest in what they've already done—even if it was just yesterday! The searchlight of their attention is directed by their fascination with what might happen, what could happen, and what is beginning to happen. This can be a disadvantage in situations requiring them to look back and reflect. It can easily feel like an unwelcome effort!

WHAT'S YOUR DEFAULT SETTING?

What are the sort of indicators that tell you whether you are procedural or inventive?

Here are some ideas—see which column fits you most:

Procedural	Inventive
Reliable	Likes new things, places, people
Tidy	
Methodical	Enjoys experimenting
Seeks information before making decisions	May tend to start things without finishing them
Rehearses things in advance	Not concerned about challenge or changing direction
Makes plans	
Respects authority and expertise	Impatient of routines or stick-in-the-mud people
Cautious about new experiences	
Comfortable with habits (dress, tastes, food and drink, holiday venues)	Doesn't hang on to the past just because it is the past
	Likes to explore (places, activities, friendships, cuisine, new projects)
Loyal to friends, places	

chart continues on next page ➤

Procedural	Inventive
May stay in the same career	May take pride in having own style (perhaps idiosyncratic)
Consistent values	
Can be anxious about the unfamiliar or new	May change employment more than once—career grows organically not sequentially
May prefer avoiding challenge	Seeks stimulus
	Feels trapped by routines or bored by them

THE BEST OF BOTH WORLDS

It's important to recognize that a procedural person isn't "petty" or "rigid" in their thinking any more than an inventive person is "disorganized," "chaotic" or "unsystematic." Both are approaching things in the way that feels natural and most appropriate from their perspective. As with any meta-program contrast, the challenge is to trust that the other person's view is just as valid as your own! In fact, the two approaches are often complementary.

Choosing procedures

Procedural approaches are most useful when you want to replicate something that already works, or if you want to understand why something doesn't work. Repeatability is built into procedures, which is why they are reliable in a situation where none of the variables has changed.

Choosing inventiveness

Where you are dealing with a new situation, where something has changed in a familiar one, or where precedents are

Using "modeling" to benefit from procedures

Procedures are at the heart of some of the fundamental discoveries of NLP. When you start to look at how an excellent practitioner in any field does what they do (which includes how they think as well as how they act) you are seeking out the procedures they use. NLP calls this "modeling." Modeling how something is done well gives you the essential information to do it better yourself. Modeling how something is done badly shows you the pitfalls to avoid. And, of course, you can model your own ways of creating success and failure as a way of doing more of the first and avoiding the second. Modeling is explained more fully in Chapter 13.

lacking, an inventive approach is your best way forward. Your watchword in these situations is: do something different.

Flexibility matters

You can benefit from being procedural without being a procedural person, and you can benefit from inventiveness without making it your way of living. A friend of ours is brilliant at sewing without a pattern. When she bought a dress that didn't fit properly, she was determined to use it for something because she loved the fabric, so she took it apart and made a fitted vest. I have never had that kind of confidence in my sewing, although many years ago I did make designer clothes for myself and my husband, including ambitious projects like overcoats and jackets. I knew that I didn't have the skill to manage without guidance, so I bought designer patterns—many of them very complex with upward of a hundred steps to carry out. I knew that, despite my lack of experience, carefully following expert procedures would help me create stylish clothing for a low cost.

By definition, once something has been invented it may then become the basis of a procedure. Designers of original or boutique items often sell their designs as drawings or as unique items. Once the customer has bought the idea, a procedure for making it (or making multiples of it) will then have to be devised. A one-off may take huge amounts of time to construct but, if copies are to be made, someone will have to work out methods of small- or large-scale manufacturing that are economical and repeatable. One recent example was that of a young mother who found ways to decorate her children's Croc sandals. Their friends liked them and wanted to decorate theirs. She realized she had stumbled on a good business idea and started getting her decorations manufactured in bulk. Pretty soon she was running a successful company. Her product was based on something original, yet it was now widely available.

The surgeon who invented the non-surgical method of correcting club feet, Dr. Ignacio Ponseti, bypassed the established treatment and developed a non-invasive and more successful treatment. He combined a procedural precision learned during childhood in his father's watch-making workshop with an inventive application of what was known about bone development in the womb to arrive at a process of manipulation followed by "serial casting" to gradually realign the foot through a series of adjustments. The solution he arrived at resulted from combining the inventiveness of a new way of looking at the problem with the reliability and precision of a procedure to correct it.

One of the messages of this book is that we all need to become somewhat inventive with respect to ourselves, because if we don't experiment at the edges of our comfort zones and don't try stretching toward the opposite ends of our different programs we will be stuck with the disadvantages of our habitual assumptions and habitual behavior.

Here are some quick aide-mémoire for helping you become more flexible in your thinking.

If you are procedural, you are	If you are inventive, you are
Naturally convergent in your thinking. When you find one solution ask yourself, "What else?"	Someone who looks for multiple solutions. Ask, "What criteria will help me decide which is best?"
Hugely responsible. Ask, "Is this really up to me?"	Task-focused. Ask, "Are other people taken care of?"
A perfectionist. Ask, "Just how perfect does this really need to be?"	Experimental. Ask, "Has anything vital been left out?"
Careful, detailed and sequential. Ask, "Does this really require this much detail?"	Someone who enjoys the process of inventing in its own right. Ask, "What actually needs to be achieved and completed here?"

BRAIN-BUILDING EXERCISES

EXERCISE 1 *What's missing?*

This exercise gets you to take advantage of the opposite way of doing things while continuing to think in your familiar, comfortable way. It honors your natural meta-program position while giving you access to the benefits of its opposite.

➤

- **If you are a procedural person**, you can gain some of the benefits of inventiveness by giving yourself another procedure to follow. You just add another procedure on to the ones that come naturally to you—only this procedure is an inventive one! It's simple: every time you are about to use an established procedure to help you do a task, ask yourself, "Is there another way?" And every time you think you've solved a problem, ask yourself, "What other solutions might there be?" You are giving yourself a new, tried-and-tested procedure that can actually deliver some of the advantages of being inventive.

- **If you are an inventive person**, you do the same kind of thing in reverse. Every time you are about to do something, ask yourself, "Have I thought of everything?" "Everything" is a good word for inventive people to use, because it latches on to your expansive way of thinking, while at the same time including the kinds of things you don't naturally think of, like risks and safety checks and unintended consequences. Having solved your problem or completed your task, you can ask yourself another question: "Is this task likely to crop up again? If so, is this the kind of thing that's really worth spending my creativity on in the future? If not, would I be prepared to jot down how I did it so as to save my creative energy for things more worthy of it?"

EXERCISE 2 *Doing it differently*

When I was doing my NLP training we were asked to think of something we would like to be able to do better. Then we had to pair up with someone who found that thing easy,

➤

and find out how they went about it. I wanted to learn how to manage my finances better, until I learned from my "expert" that she did it by means of daily records and weekly–monthly budgets. Then I knew just why I found it difficult! But what I did learn from the exercise was that if I wanted to be better at something I found difficult, I would have to modify my approach. That's what this exercise is about.

1. Do you know someone who would approach the same problem very differently from you? If so, thinking about how they would do it can give you additional, and different, strategies to use. There are a number of things you can do to learn from their way of going about things.

2. Pick a task. It could be something inherently procedural or inventive. Everyday examples might include writing thank-you letters, sending Christmas cards in good time, thinking of a fun place to go on holiday, starting a conversation at a party, keeping things tidy at work or at home, redecorating a room, and so on.

3. What are you likely to find easy about this task? If you think you're going to do it well, just how will you be going about it? Jot down some notes (or make a mental video or scenario that helps you remember).

4. Imagine how your "opposite partner" would go about the same task. What would be the differences between you?

5. If you are able to have a conversation with this person, "interview" them about how they would do it.

6. What could you learn from their approach? What might they learn from yours?

HOW THEY DO IT

Su Reid, university lecturer

66 I never cook from a recipe without changing it. I never wear a dress, but always a top and trousers (very occasionally a skirt!), so that I can invent new combinations most days. I absolutely can't be bothered to remember directions involving road numbers. In fact, I can't really be bothered with numbers at all, or at least not with doing routine sums. But when writing a lecture or planning a meeting, or even writing an article for publication, I know that I have to work out a clear progressing agenda, and stick to it. Working it out can be laborious, because I so easily interrupt myself with yet another new idea; but once the agenda is there I am liberated! I can write or talk with energy because I don't have to decide what I'm heading for. I've done that already. 99

CHAPTER **5**

How Do You Experience Time?

One of NLP's most interesting discoveries was that everyone's experience of time is spatial: we literally locate ourselves within it as within a physical dimension. The way we position ourselves in relation to our individual "timeline" creates different possibilities and problems, as Tad James and Wyatt Woodsmall explored in their 1988 book *Time Line Therapy and the Basis of Personality*. Even if different individuals share the concept of time as a line between past and future, they experience that line as laid out differently in space, and place themselves differently in relation to it. Time, in other words, is not a fixed, "out-there" entity but rather an individual mental construction.

Most people are not aware that they are doing this. They tend to assume that time just is, and that any one person's life consists of going along as though they were following a piece of string. Yet when you actually ask people to explain in more detail how they personally experience the passage of time and how they perceive their relationship to it, you discover that there are many different ways!

LIVING IN THE HERE AND NOW vs. TAKING AN OVERVIEW

We are all orienteering through time, just as we might seek to find our way through a physical landscape, and so we each experience time quite idiosyncratically. But somehow we assume everyone's experience is much the same! In reality, we are mapping time differently from each other.

If you don't know how you are doing something, or assume that everyone does something the same way, you don't realize that you have any choice in the matter. Knowing that time can be mapped differently opens up the possibility of evaluating how effective your familiar map is and of asking what you might gain from mapping differently.

HOW DO YOU "MAP" TIME?

If you ask someone to point toward last week, or toward the future, they may be surprised, or even amused, but once they have gotten over their surprise at being asked such an odd question they will usually point without hesitation in specific, and contrasting, directions. There are many individual variations, but experiencing time usually runs according to one of two common patterns. As you read, you may find one of these is "your way"; but variations and combinations are not uncommon, so if neither quite seems to fit, try to pinpoint exactly how you do experience it. Knowing the details of your own filtering pattern will help you customize the brain-building exercises so that they better serve your needs.

BEING "THROUGH-TIME"

This way of experiencing comes closest to the piece-of-string analogy, and has been called "through-time" because through-time experiencers feel as though time is "laid out" in a side-to-side manner just in front of them, being both continuous and visually accessible. These people will usually point to one side of them for the past and to the other side for the future. Most commonly, past is to the left and future is to the right. (Sometimes the line from the past runs from the side but then bends ahead of the person's present toward the future.) When they are talking casually about events, or planning them, their hands may also gesture sideways, often even indicating a specific direction. They may talk about "having an overview" or a "long view."

Advantages and disadvantages

Having time "spread out" before you means that you can, quite literally, take an "overview" of it. Usually your now is located somewhere roughly equidistant between past and future on your timeline. Because of this, you will probably find it easy to make plans and check out consequences. You understand how the past affects the present, and can make a fair estimate of how both could affect the future. The disadvantage of a through-time perspective is that you may not really feel "in" or "part of" your experiences, but slightly or even substantially distanced from them. That seems to be the penalty you pay for your ability to "take a long view."

BEING "IN-TIME"

In-time experiencers are located on a timeline that runs continuously from behind them (past) and out ahead of them. If you are one of them, you can't see the past because it's behind you. This may make it difficult for you to refer back to it (note the word "back"!), or to "think forward" very far (the further away in the future something is, the more it will be obscured by what is closer to you). You will tend to be immersed in your experience: your good times are really good; your bad times are really bad; fun is great; misery, disappointment, frustration can seem overwhelming. Even if you know such feelings won't last, it doesn't feel like that "right now." Because you are so "in" it, time may pass like a flash, or it may seem to slow right down and lengthen out.

Advantages and disadvantages

Life feels very immediate and real to you. You have no trouble "getting lost" in a book or being "caught up in" an experience. You can probably switch off and relax just as easily as you can get involved and excited. On the other hand, you may tend to be so involved in what you are doing that you overrun the time available and are late for what comes next. Time just seems to get away from you! This may mean that you get distracted, so that you don't do what you intended, or find it takes much longer than you expected. You may have wonderful goals for the day, the year, or indeed for your life, but dismay yourself because you never quite get around to achieving them. "Where did the day go?" you may wonder. You may find it difficult to talk yourself out of anxieties, because they are overwhelmingly real at the time, and a future in which things will get better seems vague and far off. Equally, in your enthusiasm about something or someone right now you may jump in headfirst. Assessing consequences does not come easy to you, so mistakes can be hard to avoid.

During the most acute phase of the 2008 financial meltdown, one of my clients working in a merchant bank heard a senior manager proposing to colleagues that they should look three years ahead to help them develop strategies to come through the other side. "We can't look that far ahead" was the anguished response. "We need to find a solution now!" The market analyst George Soros pointed out the danger of such a short-term (in-time) view of the catastrophe. He argued:

With the financial system in cardiac arrest, resuscitating it took precedence over considerations of moral hazard—i.e. the danger that coming to the rescue of a financial institution in difficulties would reward and encourage reckless behavior in the future—and the authorities injected ever larger quantities of money.

New York Review of Books

If we take an overview (through-time), we can see that the same mental map that had seemed to serve operators in the markets—immediate, reactive, quick-response, in-time, facilitating rapid decision-making of the buy-or-sell kind—had blinded them to the possible longer-term systemic implications; and, more seriously, the methodological inadequacies of the model that said that markets are self-correcting, which eventually led to the crisis.

WHAT'S YOUR DEFAULT SETTING?

If you are through-time	If you are in-time
Your feelings are more considered.	You wear your heart on your sleeve.
You see what you're doing in a wider context.	You get involved in what you're doing.
You are usually on time. You learn from the past, and connect now to the future.	Time slips by—punctuality is a problem. You put bad times and bad things behind you.
You are good at future planning. You find it easy to work toward goals.	You don't easily think very far ahead. You find it difficult to work toward long-term goals.
You use phrases like "overview," "overall," "process."	You use phrases like "put it behind me," "look forward to it."

THE BEST OF BOTH WORLDS

We need to be able to manage time from both perspectives, and to know which is most appropriate and when. Many things in life benefit from wholehearted involvement in the moment: pleasure, attending to others and learning are some examples. When we're engaged in any of these, it would indeed be a pity to have half our minds elsewhere. Even unpleasant experiences, such as loss, disappointment or pain, are best attended to before we attempt to soften them or change them in any way. Ignoring them diminishes their vital signal value. We need to appreciate their nature and their impact if we are to take appropriate action.

On the other hand, if we get lost in the moment we can miss out on an important connection it may have to the past and the future—and we have no alternative perspective on it. This is the primary value of through-time: it puts the present in a context. It makes it possible to learn from mistakes rather than burying them or being destroyed by them; it allows us to anticipate a time when pain or sorrow may diminish; it allows us to plan in a way that makes it possible to realize our dreams.

BRAIN-BUILDING EXERCISES

Trying out a different way of orienteering in time is likely to feel strange, perhaps initially even uncomfortable, just because it is different from what you're used to. You may be surprised to feel anything at all, of course, because your usual way of experiencing time is so ingrained that it feels natural and therefore comfortable. You take it for granted. If you do feel different as you do the exercises, that tells you that you are indeed stretching and strengthening yourself.

EXERCISE 1 *Discovering different timelines*

As you play with aligning time differently, and experiment with moving along timelines, you will experience a range of feelings that are part physical and part emotional: relaxation, ease, tension, confusion, amusement, even perhaps a sense of freedom and delight. Provided the extent of any feeling seems acceptable, continue with the exercise and treat your responses as a good source of additional information. If any feeling should concern you, stop the exercise, reorient your timeline to its usual alignment, and then ask yourself what was going on there. Feelings always give us useful information, so taking time to reflect can in itself add to your learning.

1. In a relatively open space (the sitting room or office, if uncluttered, or a public space such as a park) think of how your usual timeline is laid out. Note where you are standing, or mark it with a piece of paper, and then find visual markers for your past and future. Imagine your timeline stretching between them.

2. Find markers for the other timeline layout.

3. Think of the events of yesterday, today and tomorrow (or this week if you prefer) according to your usual timeline. Then imagine them laid out according to the alternative timeline. This may feel strange or even uncomfortable at first, but persevere. Remind yourself that this is only a way of thinking and that you can change back if and when you want to. You could walk beside your timeline into your past or into the future, stepping onto it in order to locate yourself at any specific time you want to get the feel of. Use this technique with caution, as stepping into

➤

traumatic or saddening times can heighten their impact and is best avoided unless you have qualified support.

4. Ask yourself what happens when you organize your understanding of time differently. What is easier/more difficult when you switch? In what ways do your feelings and thoughts change? What new information do you get from experiencing time this way?

5. Experiment. Practice changing your timeline from one orientation to another until you can do it easily and without discomfort. Practice doing it just in your head, without the use of external reference points. Your objective is to become more flexible, so that you can apply both orientations appropriately according to your situation and needs, and derive both sets of benefits. When would it benefit you to be in-time? When would it be more useful to be through-time?

Planning with through-time: relaxing with in-time

Application 1 When planning engagements or arrangements, whether work or personal, set up a through-time orientation for yourself to check what needs doing when, how much time you need, whether you can meet any deadlines, how tired you may feel, and so on. Don't forget holidays and Christmas—it's amazing how stressful it can be to get ready for a holiday if you haven't planned the winding-down and finishing-up beforehand, and how much pressure there is over Christmas to see everyone, get everything ready, live with disrupted domestic patterns (and perhaps also with

➤

disrupting relations!) and even just survive all the parties and feasts! Some people find it helpful to begin the week, or even each day, with a brief through-time planning and review session with themselves, before going in-time for the more interactive part of the day.

Application 2 When you are about to do something fun or you want to relax, check that you are in-time so that you can make the most of it. If you find you are distracted at any point by thinking about something outside the situation, close your eyes briefly and switch your timeline around in your head—imagine changing its orientation as you might change a ruler from pointing across your body to straddling yourself over it back and front. Then just enjoy!

EXERCISE 2 *Leap-frog*

If you are experiencing a problem, taking a through-time orientation will help you understand it in context. But if you are naturally in-time, you could also try leap-frogging the problem.

1. Walk briskly up your timeline to somewhere in your future where your problem has either gone away or been solved. Your body will tell you when you have gotten there, because you will feel an almost immediate sense of relaxation or relief.

2. Ask yourself what has changed. How did the problem get solved? (If solving the problem was done by others, ask yourself what you did that brought it to their notice or assisted them in helping you to change it. This strategy

➤

is about your actions; you can't have a strategy for winning the lottery!)

3. Turn around and walk slowly back to the present, noticing each point along the way where you took any actions that helped solve the problem. Once in the present again, turn around again to face your future and notice how differently you feel now that you know you can solve the problem—and how! When will you take that first important step?

HOW DO YOU VALUE THE FUTURE AND THE PAST?

Orienteers use their equipment to navigate through unfamiliar territory. When we are orienteering in time we are guided by our purposes and our values. In the Western world, for example, we are used to assuming a culturally ingrained "value-add" of progress: we tend to believe that as the years and the centuries go by, things get better. Medicine and technology make advances. Civilization develops. This means that we "look forward" to better times. Illness sufferers demand that the latest drugs be made available to them because they believe that latest means best—a belief shared by the drug manufacturers, although not always borne out in use over time.

Like most people, I had not questioned this value-laden assumption about the passage of time, and I was unaware that the map it offered for the understanding of evolution and history was a partial, and therefore inherently distorting, one. But some years ago I read a fascinating book about China called *The Tyranny of History*, which made me realize how blinkered I was. The author, W. J. F. Jenner, describes how the

Chinese have both a reverence for the past and a cultural habit of referring to a huge body of stories that seem like timeless variations on recurring themes, which together act to blur a sense of history as something that people go through. He says:

> The whole traditional culture encouraged one to face antiquity, to look toward the past . . . and to assume that older generally meant better . . . the rule that thou shalt commit no novelty, unless it can be hidden or else disguised as a reversion to something from the past that has since been lost.
>
> *The Tyranny of History*, pp. 8–9

This contrast with the Western conceptualization of history could hardly be greater, and clearly has major implications for world trade and politics. In terms of mental flexibility, however, we can take from this contrast the understanding that believing in "progress" is just as narrow a view as an extreme reverence for all that has gone.

We are accustomed to thinking of the Dark Ages of English history as a primitive, war-ridden, tribal time. Yet you have only to look at the artifacts found in the Sutton Hoo ship burial and displayed in the British Museum, or the Alfred Jewel on show in Oxford's Ashmolean Museum, to be astounded by workmanship as technically accomplished as any that the most sophisticated modern workshop and the most subtle of designers could produce. Even when we marvel at their achievements, we take, I think, the patronizing view that the makers were achieving something amazing in spite of their circumstances. How would it change our understanding of the past if we thought that their circumstances were an essential, causative, part of their achievements?

Assuming that the passage of time favors "progress" inclines us toward accepting social or technological "advances" (again, the words are a giveaway!) without assessing their implications as critically as we might.

If you assume that knowledge and technology advance over time, you may tend to assume that the more recent a discovery or the later a model is, the better it will be in relation to its predecessors. You may also assume that as people get older they may acquire wisdom from experience but are less likely to be up with cutting-edge information. If, on the other hand, you assume that tradition is the custodian of excellence, you may be suspicious of change and feel that "the country is going to the dogs." In both cases you are likely to find evidence to support your opinion!

EXERCISE 3 *Shifting your value-loading*

The essence of this exercise is to surface the assumptions you are currently making and check them for unconscious bias.

1. Find "now" on your timeline. (For this exercise, it doesn't much matter whether you are in- or through-time.) You may find that it helps to write the word "now" on a piece of paper, put it in your "now" spot and stand on it.

2. Now think of something you value negatively. If it is in the present, place it beside you by writing a word or description of it on another piece of paper.

3. Staying in the present, turn to face the past. Does your negative valuation change when you consider your chosen item in the light of all that has preceded it and, if so, in what way?

4. Now turn to face the future. Does your valuation change in any way when you consider it in relation to what is yet to come?

➤

5. Move off your "now" spot by a step or two, while remaining in your present. If you are through-time you can do this by backing up a little from your usual position in relation to your timeline. If you are in-time you can just step slightly to one side. You are likely to feel a little strange, because you have taken up, even though temporarily, a position slightly displaced from your usual one. How does this shift affect the way you value your chosen item?

6. Now step back onto your "now" spot, taking up the orientation you are used to, and bringing all this enriched information with you. You will probably find that your valuation is more complex and more thoughtful. Does it prompt you to act differently in any way?

HOW THEY DO IT

Sylvia Tute, NHS program manager

66 I am naturally an in-time person, with my focus in the here and now and my timeline running from the past behind me to the future in front. But I can also strategize and plan. It is as if I am hovering above a center point that is the present so that events and plans appear to be laid out like a map. Important things to come lie to the north with dates like milestones. Those that have already happened are arranged to the south, and other things that I am less closely involved with move along on either side. That makes it easy to see what I am aiming for and what needs to happen for me to get there, and to see where I have come from. Then I know I can drop down into the present again and make sure it all gets done. 99

CHAPTER **6**

How Emotional Do You Get?

Stuff just happens to us, doesn't it? Well, not necessarily. There are two contrasting ways to manage experience: you can become fully involved emotionally, or you can maintain a degree of distance from it.

It's clear that we don't all experience the same event in the same way. Some people show signs of panic or distress at injuries, accidents or disappointments. Others manage to keep calm in very similar circumstances. How do they do that? Yet that very same "together" person may in different circumstances jitter about making a decision or agonize about something that wouldn't disturb someone else at all. What is going on to create such differences, both between people and within the same person at different times?

REGULATING CLOSENESS vs. DISTANCE

There's a meta-program at work here. Its polar opposites are being emotionally involved or present in what you're experiencing on the one hand and being emotionally distanced or remote from it on the other. Emotional involvement is referred to as being associated (that is, personally connected), and emotional distancing is known as being dissociated. The key idea is *connection*, which also forms the basis of the brain-building exercises at the end of this chapter.

YOUR RELATIONSHIP TO EXPERIENCE

Although most young children seem emotionally involved in what they are doing, they begin quite soon to learn that they can also take a more detached view of what's going on. It may be that the ability to detach emotionally goes hand in hand with learning to analyze or comment on experience rather than just having it. By the time most people reach adulthood, they have a fair degree of ability to choose whether to be immersed in an experience or more distant from it. Yet, even here, people do seem to have natural default positions somewhere between the polar extremes.

Are you immersed in your experiences, or more detached from them? Is your relationship to your experiences the way you want or need them to be? This is a choice you will be exercising even as you read this chapter. Notice from time to time whether it touches your feelings or whether your responses are predominantly objective and intellectual.

Association and dissociation are both mind–body "states," each with its own characteristic pattern of breathing, heart rate and metabolic rate.

State A constellation of mind–body factors at any one time. The totality of how you are at any given moment.

Do we always have a choice?

Some emotions are so powerful that virtually everyone finds themselves actively drawn into experiencing them—this is probably because they get us into survival mode really fast. Most people find their heart rate speeds up when they are excited and when they're frightened, and that this is as true whether the stimulus is emotional or physical. Apart from extreme situations, during any one day we may be more or less involved in our experience but, just as with the other meta-program, it is also the case that each of us has a natural default setting somewhere between involvement and distancing. Each one of us will experience our own personal "bundle" of linked emotional/physical phenomena when we are associated and a different one when we are dissociated.

Physical feeling

You could think of being involved or distant from what is going on as a matter of having more or less "feeling" about it; but feelings aren't things that only happen in the mind. People vary in how strongly they connect to their experience, and they also vary in the way their bodies manifest what they feel. For some people, stress involves their digestion: they may feel sick, need to go to the bathroom frequently or lose their appetite—or all of these. When I was little, I experienced these same sensations not only when I was worried or anxious but also when I was excited—before a party, for example.

These clusters of symptoms are not the results of associated feelings, but an essential part of them. Their onset is at once evidence of a change of state and a manifestation of it. Attempting to change the physical symptoms can help break the pattern. Beta-blockers, for example, can lower blood pressure and make people feel calmer, but this is rarely enough in the longer term, because the physical experience is part of the emotional response. Beta-blockers can help cut through a pattern of stress, but they can't change what causes it. For that you have to change the situation or alter the way you feel about it.

BEING ASSOCIATED

"Wholehearted" is a word that describes this state well. It contains the sense of immersion and the feeling of whole-being involvement that characterize associated response.

Advantages

If things are exciting, stimulating, enjoyable, or even just pleasant, it seems good to experience them fully. That's when we're happy to be able to become drawn into the situation and experience all it has to offer us. If you are "associated into" an experience, you can pay attention to it, relish it and benefit from it more fully. You may feel especially receptive to sensory information: colors might seem brighter and richer, sensations might seem stronger or more subtle, sounds might be amplified, making for a richer and more detailed texture to your experience. That's the upside.

Disadvantages

As with any meta-program polarity, association also has its possible disadvantages. The obvious downside of association is when you are alarmed, frightened or confused: you feel at your wits' end or just plain overwhelmed. In these circumstances, being associated means you may feel you have no escape, experiencing little respite until the situation itself changes. To endure emergency conditions for a long time can be more than just unpleasant. Living with high adrenaline levels until the emergency subsides will almost certainly affect your blood pressure, your sleep, your digestion and probably your judgment, as well as your emotions. If such a high-stress state continues long enough, the body goes beyond coping into overload—a state which has the potential to cause irreversible damage, shock and even collapse.

Over the years, I have worked with a number of people who have been so associated into such feelings of anxiety and pressure that they became ill. One young man, who was excellent at his job in a multinational corporation, sat at his desk one day with his heart pounding so fast and so irregularly that he thought he was having a heart attack. Fortunately, the duty doctor at work was able to reassure him that he wasn't; but because reassurance wasn't enough to make the symptoms go away the young man's boss thought he should have some coaching sessions with me. These conversations allowed us to begin unraveling how the immediate pressures of work were picking up on and reinforcing pressures and anxieties— both past and current—from other parts of his life. Coaching helped him learn how to dissociate more, so that he could deal with the different burdens and pressures separately and more calmly. He found that he now had some choice about how he responded and how he felt.

When you are associated into feelings that threaten to overwhelm you, there are ramifications for others as well as yourself. You may react in an extreme or even inappropriate way to what is going on, and by so doing make a difficult situation even worse. Even if you "know" that the situation will pass, or that it can be coped with, this information may do little to help your feelings subside. If you are euphoric with delight, you could be similarly "insulated" from "the real world," although other people will probably be less concerned about you.

BEING DISSOCIATED

Emotional dissociation means stepping back or disengaging from feelings, and when those feelings are unpleasant it can be just as essential a survival tool as its opposite, being associated, is life-enhancing.

> 66 I know that breed . . . They think everything, think what they feel. You don't feel so fierce if you only think. Deep, this, but jolly true. They know what they'd think if anyone played such a stinker on 'em, but they don't know what the poor clot would feel because they don't. 99
>
> MARGERY ALLINGHAM, *More Work for the Undertaker*, p. 146

Advantages

People who routinely have to deal with distressing situations—for example, illness or accidents—usually develop a way of dissociating. Professional training and settings (including the use of equipment and clothing), clinical language and impersonal or routine procedures all help people such as doctors, social workers, accident crews, firemen, police and psychotherapists put a distance between their own feelings and the potential distress inherent in coping with disease, accident, trauma and death. They step out of the emotion—they dissociate. Dissociation means that they don't get caught up in patients' or victims' feelings. Dissociation allows them to remain calm so that they can use their professional skills to help people who are distressed, in pain, helpless, panicking or dying: When someone is injured, ill or anxious, they will usually feel better if whoever is helping them (a friend, doctor, therapist or lawyer, for example) is dissociated: the sufferer can relax more easily knowing that someone is calm and in control of the situation.

Dissociation is a natural human response that can evolve from experience as well as one that can be learned. People who have something important or exciting to do often don't notice physical aches, pains or even injuries while they are doing it. Most parents who have been anxious to do the best they can with a first child have at times found themselves overanxious or overprotective. Yet, eventually, they tend to discover that their infant is more robust than they at first believed! With subsequent children, this learning is usually carried forward, so they are less quick to feel worried or distressed. They reach for the damp cloth, the antibacterial cream, the Band-Aid, the thermometer, the cold remedy or the family medical encyclopedia rather than rushing immediately to the emergency room! Someone with a chronic physical problem may learn to dissociate from their discomfort (even from pain) and also from the frustration or anger it could cause. Familiarity has led them to make a choice to dissociate from these aspects of their physicality.

People who have suffered severe trauma, especially if it has been prolonged or repeated, sometimes learn to dissociate as a way of escaping emotional pain. Others who have to endure prolonged physical pain can also learn to dissociate from it to an extent. Both might sometimes report it as being like "watching myself from a distance."

Disadvantages

Dissociating from situations that would otherwise evoke strong emotions depends on having somewhere else to go in your head. It may be quite a complex process. Caring professionals will be stepping into their professional sense of identity: they will be maintaining a strong sense of separateness from the pain or suffering around them. This may have been learned initially as part of their training, but it is likely over time to have become an automatic response that happens quite unconsciously.

If someone is dissociated from your distress you may feel that they are not sympathetic, not taking your feelings seriously, or even that they are patronizing you.

The downside of dissociating from physical sensation is that you can run the risk of ignoring sensations you should really be paying attention to. Sportsmen and women can injure themselves through demanding too much physical performance from their bodies, too frequently. Because they attach so much importance to training and improved results, they may attempt to distance themselves from physical discomfort, stress and pain to their own detriment.

In other words, the short-term advantage of dissociation is also potentially a longer-term disadvantage. At its extreme, it can mean that you ignore sensations—both emotional and physical—that would be better respected and responded to.

Being associated or dissociated isn't always a simple matter of "good to be associated into nice things, better to be dissociated from sad or unpleasant ones." In real life, working out whether the response you have is useful, or appropriate, or limiting is what really matters.

Understanding other people

We are all accustomed to taking the emotional temperature of those around us, often without even consciously thinking about it; and we use this information to help build up a picture of whether they can be trusted (and for what), to predict their responses and to create strategies for interacting with them. People may consider someone who is associated most of the time to be "real" or "alive" or "volatile": they are seen as "wearing their heart on their sleeve." You may think you know where you are with them—but they may change at any moment. Even if they don't change, someone whose feelings are close to the surface may not be the person you want to turn to in a crisis, or for advice, because their response will not depend on your needs but on how they are that day. Someone who is characteristically dissociated, on the other hand, may come across as uncaring or unfeeling, even if this is not actually the case.

HOW THE BODY STATES ARE TRIGGERED

To be able to manage yourself and others effectively, it helps to understand how these mind–body states of association and dissociation are triggered. Both associated and dissociated states can be induced by external triggers, known as anchors.

> **Anchor** A stimulus or trigger for a particular state. Anchors are sensory based: any smell, sight, sound, taste or sensation can become linked in the mind to a specific state such as anxiety, excitement, fear or inward contemplation. When the stimulus occurs again it will reinduce the state it was previously linked with.

Anchors are strongly implicated in recurring trauma, anxiety and fear, but they can be just as much a part of pleasure and excitement. Being associated and being dissociated can be triggered by specific anchors, as well as being part of someone's characteristic way of responding to life.

Sudden switching of state

Being upset on the one hand, or calm or excited on the other, doesn't automatically follow from what is actually happening. Most people have at one time or another experienced an unexpected change of state. One minute you were averagely contented, yet a few minutes later you noticed you were feeling slightly flat or even sad. What was that about? Equally, there may have been times when you were surprised not to be experiencing strong feelings: for example, finding yourself remaining calm in the midst of a family or office conflict. How did you manage to feel so uninvolved and remote?

Even if you think events are plunging you straight into an emotional state with no moment of pause, something important and powerful actually comes between event and response. To create or change a mind–body state, a trigger is needed—known in NLP as an anchor. As the image suggests, anchors have things attached to them: they are linking mechanisms—individual phenomena that connect to particular memories, feelings or responses.

The connection may be—and indeed, often is—quite coincidental rather than logical. Incidental features of a situation are registered unconsciously as part of the whole, and any one of them can later act as an anchor that precipitates feelings similar to those felt the "first time round." For example, a song that was playing in the background of a special meeting can become "our song" regardless of its words or tempo. A piece of clothing you happened to be wearing when you won that vital game or had that successful job interview can afterward appear to bring good fortune. Even though you "know" that wearing it has no logical effect on the outcome of future tests and challenges you still choose to wear it in the future as a kind of talisman to help set up success. And, of course, it does have the power to do that: it can influence outcomes precisely because it changes your state, thus changing how you feel and how you are able to act.

As a psychotherapist, I quite often encountered people affected by humiliating or criticizing anchors. There are plenty of "good" anchors, too. For most people, birthdays and anniversaries are anchors for pleasant feelings, because the dates are attached to pleasant memories of being spoiled, feeling special and receiving presents. The first signs of spring often stimulate many people to feel livelier and more cheerful. Christmas can be a powerful anchor, although it's not always a pleasant one. For some people it can anchor feelings of stress as well as—or even instead of—those of excitement.

Many writers deliberately inaugurate their own creative states through the incidental anchors provided by features of their workrooms. Examples include neat rows of pencils ready sharpened each night to set up the next day's work, special colored notepads, garden sheds free from distraction, even a sleeping bag to provide warmth and comfort while writing.

Anchors can bring about dissociated states, too. The professional self of nurses, police officers and other helpers can be "brought online" by physical anchors such as professional clothing, technical jargon and the mental anchors of other people's spoken or implied expectations. For most people, going to work is in itself an anchor, which activates a specialized part of themselves, rather than their full, complex self.

THE BEST OF BOTH WORLDS

Association and dissociation can both be useful states for responding to life's events when appropriate to the circumstances and when the state enriches your experience rather than overwhelming you, depleting your energies or limiting your ability to think and act effectively. The detective story writer Donna Leon describes her hero and his wife as having contrasting "takes" on emotion, although her novels make it clear that within their marriage these are usually complementary and enriching:

Paola usually opted for light and the forward leap into life, while his spirit felt more comfortable one step back from the stage, where things were less well illuminated and he could study them and adjust his vision before deciding what to do.

Willful Behavior, pp. 257–8

Recognizing what anchors or triggers these two states helps you to manage yourself effectively in relation to the needs of the situations you're in. Training yourself to observe other people closely can help you spot the precise moment when an anchor or trigger affects them. Usually this will be their expression, their stance or their gestures and often even the color of their skin will change immediately. If you are alert for changes, you can reflect on what might have caused them. Was it something you said? Was it a change of topic? Was it something in the background that might have caught their attention unconsciously and affected how they were feeling?

Once you have noticed a change, simply commenting on it can be helpful. "You looked puzzled then. Would it help if I explained again?" or "I'm so sorry, have I upset you?" By describing what you see and acknowledging that the physical change in the other person may be reflecting a change in their state, you are getting them to reflect on themselves, which in turn helps them dissociate from the (negative) emotions you have seen reflected. This can also happen if you comment on changes that seem to indicate they are associating into a more pleasant state—your comments may in fact serve to reinforce the new state.

BRAIN-BUILDING EXERCISES

As you were reading this section, some parts of the descriptions probably seemed to describe you more than others. By now, it's likely that you've recognized your default position as primarily associated or dissociated or, alternatively, you may have found that you can vary depending on the circumstances. You might be more toward the dissociated end of the spectrum when you're at work, for example, and more associated when you're with your family. You might be very associated when you're taking part in a competitive sport or doing something like cooking, gardening, writing or painting. You may find it useful to jot down your own pattern of responses. You could start now with anything that occurs to you, and perhaps add to your mini-profile anything else that occurs to you over the next few days or weeks.

EXERCISE 1 *Does your default setting work for you or is it limiting you?*

Do you get really mad when you're driving and someone else tailgates you or cuts in? However justified your response may seem to be, the very fact that you get so mad probably means that your judgment is being clouded by being so associated. At a weekend or on holiday, do you find it difficult to let go and play? If so, it may be that you are being inhibited in your leisure time by the very dissociation that helps you stay focused and efficient at work.

1. In which situations do you feel your state truly matches the situation and helps you respond to it appropriately? Jot down your answers.

2. In another column, or on another page, jot down those situations in which your state isn't serving you so well.

EXERCISE 2 *Closeness and distance*

Using the idea of closeness and distance, and taking different examples from your everyday life, experiment with increasing/decreasing the degree of your association/dissociation in order to create the best game between your state and what's needed in the situation.

Association and dissociation, like all mind–body states, are quite strongly physical, which is why it can help to do this exercise standing and moving in space. It is surprising how immediate and powerful learning can be when it is made physical in this way. (If you are not able to move around freely, start by imagining a space you know well where you could move freely in either direction—perhaps in a large, uncluttered room, or on a path in a quiet park or public space, and do your moving around in your mind.)

1. In an open or relatively clear space imagine a line or continuum between association on the one hand and dissociation on the other. Note where the ends are. (You will probably find that it's immediately clear which end stands for which state. If in doubt, just give them opposite designations.) For the moment, stand clear of the line but close to it, somewhere toward the midway point.

2. Think of a situation (work or non-work) where you feel confident that you are or were in an appropriate and effective state. Immediately head for the line and step onto it, noticing where you now stand in relation to each extreme. (You are probably no longer at the midway point!) Spend a moment or two reflecting on that experience in order to learn just how your state helped, or helps, you in managing it.

➤

3. Step off the line again and resume your midway station.

4. Now think of another situation where you feel you are less well placed to manage effectively. (Avoid any situations where you feel you manage really badly—these are best tackled with outside help.)

5. Step onto the line, at the place that feels most natural to you. You will probably be closer to one polar extreme than the other. Notice how you feel, placed at that point, about the situation.

6. Now take a couple of steps along the line in the direction of the opposite extreme. If you are becoming more associated, you may find your feelings are more involved or more enhanced. If you are moving toward greater dissociation, you may find your responses are becoming more impersonal and emotionally low-key. You might also find that you want to move even closer to the end you naturally operate from (for example, to enjoy something by being even more involved, or to be even cooler and more impersonal about something). Stop after a couple of steps to assess the difference you have made. Do you want to go any further at this point? It is possible that you may prefer to get used to a slight difference before making one that's any greater. You can always repeat the exercise and push your learning still further on another day.

7. Step off the line and resume your midway point. Jot down what you have noticed and anything that has occurred to you about what anchors your old response.

8. If your move has seemed useful, what might serve as an anchor for your new position? Step back onto the line

➤

in the new position, letting yourself notice things that might serve as an anchor in future.

9. Test a new anchor off-line by just thinking about it. Does it immediately put you in the state you desire? Does it make you want to step back on the line in the new place?

Stepping on and off the meta-program line and deliberately changing your placing on it like this can be illuminating and powerful, whether your movement is imagined or actual. Its effects aren't limited to the insights you receive while you are actually doing the exercise but can often set off trains of thought that may bear fruit later on.

HOW THEY DO IT

Helen Vaughan, senior nurse

❝While managing potentially distressing situations in the hospital, I'm careful not to put communication barriers up by being too 'professional' (clichés are a big no-no). I watch for clues in body language and follow gut instinct (to touch or not touch). At the back of my mind is always the question 'How would I want to be treated?' Invest time in communicating at either a superficial or deep level, i.e., making regular update phone calls to relatives of ill or dying patients. Talk/phone if a problem arises—delays let things fester. If you make the links (I imagine a bridge, or reaching out of hands) early, it is much easier to deal with bad news later, because you've already made/built a relationship and settled on assumptions that don't have to be worked

➤

through at the same time as making sense of a complex event/discussion.

I don't expend energy on trying to hide my emotions—I don't think you can plausibly demonstrate empathy without showing some emotion. I focus—at that moment in time—on maintaining calm/balance (which might reflect sadness rather than distress, or disappointment rather than anger), and offering honest responses (as opposed to meaning-less platitudes). I am a sponge that can absorb. I dissipate (wring out!) by sorting through my thoughts later; away from the situation (in the car with loud music or running with loud music). Occasionally the sponge is actually a fragile egg threatening to crack. I have tried visualizing the screw-ing up of thoughts into balls of paper to chuck in the bin, but find a better distraction is visualizing a walk through my house and imagining the transformations I would do if I won the lottery. Failing that, brandy and a good book in bed. 99

CHAPTER **7**

Who Influences Your Judgments?

Our choices and decisions are driven, or directed, by a sense of what is right or appropriate. Some people look outside themselves for authority, others look within themselves. Whenever you make a decision that involves some kind of value judgment, you are basing it on a standard or belief you carry in your head. Every time you think or say words like "better," "right," "good," "appropriate," "wise," "sensible," "advantageous" (or, of course, their opposites), you are referring back to an implied standard, whether or not you are aware of its presence or conscious of referring to it. This baseline standard is what directs you.

RELYING ON YOURSELF vs. OTHERS

Where does that implied standard come from? Whose opinion are you referring—or deferring—to? Are you looking outside yourself, or inward, for the criteria on which to base your thoughts and actions?

When I was training as a therapist, one of our teachers used to tell us about some of his recent clients and the issues they were struggling with. Then he'd ask us to brainstorm about them: what would we do in his place? As we hesitated and wondered how to reply, his characteristic instruction was: "Quick, quick—think on your feet!" I have found that to be a really helpful mantra over the years. I now realize that's because it fits with and reinforces my inner-directedness! But if I had been someone who tended to look to others, or to established procedures, for answers, I might well have felt anxious or even abandoned by my teacher instead of energized and liberated.

Someone who looks to themselves for guidance is described as being "inner-directed." If you look to others for guidance you are "outer-directed." Being "outer-directed" or "inner-directed" is not a matter of what you do. It's more a matter of how you make the decision to do it. A deeply religious person might be outer-directed, loyally working within historic tradition or, on the other hand, inner-directed, finding fulfillment and purpose in creating new ways to express and serve their religious vision.

BEING OUTER-DIRECTED

If you are outer-directed, an important source of your sense of direction is what you have been explicitly told by other people, especially adults who were important to you during your early childhood and formal education. Their power, authority and knowledge, their greater experience of living, gave them the "right" to tell you, and led you to accept what they said. As you go about your daily life, they will be your internal mentors, guiding your actions, your choices and your decisions, whether or not you realize it. Some of these people accompany you in your daily routines and daily choices, from how you boil your breakfast egg to how you organize your day, as well as in the apparently more significant choices you make about friends, partners, jobs, hobbies and parenting.

It's not just their words that influence you. What they did and how they did it are there in your mind as well, making up an endless audio-visual-somatic reference bank. Sometimes you dip into it deliberately—*what would Dad have thought about this?* Sometimes the years of closeness you shared (or the antagonism you felt) impel you to act in this way rather than that way without even reflecting on what's influencing you.

The influence of institutions

It's not only individuals whose opinions and actions guide us: institutions such as churches, trades and professions, social groups and peer groups also contribute to our reference bank. Together, they provide us with many of the abstract criteria we use to make judgments and decisions. Some of these groupings are historical: religious traditions, national values and cultural traditions can all go back over the centuries, yet still have a powerful influence on us today.

Advantages

If you are outer-directed you will usually be pretty clear about the basis for making decisions and taking action. You may well have a strong sense of others' needs, leading you to see taking care of them as a higher priority than serving your own. You could gain great satisfaction from doing what you understand to be right, feel backed up by the ethos of roles, organizations and institutions you value, and enjoy passing on such cultural and moral values to others. You will have a sense of how you fit in, and probably of what matters in life. You feel comfortable in your culture and your community.

You might find your fulfillment in a role that involves supporting and nurturing others.

In situations of difficulty, challenge or conflict you may have a strong sense of support from your internal "mentors." You have someone (or something) to turn to. They are literally "with you" and "within you." You can tap into their wisdom, their skills, their code of conduct, to increase your own or to "speak for you." Sometimes you will even use their words or act in ways that resemble theirs.

Disadvantages

Where your authorities conflict with each other, you can be in real trouble! How can you compare them or evaluate them against each other? When their precepts don't seem to fit with the needs of a changing world, how can you tell what guidance is best to follow? By their very nature, archaic voices are not up to date, as I remember my father (a retired minister) explaining. He argued that rules for conduct that had been formulated centuries before our time to serve isolated rural communities might not necessarily translate well into the urbanized complexities of life in the 20th century. This means that he read much of the Bible's teachings as spiritual parables rather than as literal precepts.

If you are an outer-directed person and what you want or what you need to do conflicts with what you feel you ought to do or what is right, you are likely to feel very stressed. Your gut feelings and strong impulses may not necessarily harmonize with your learned beliefs. Ambition, sexual desire and instinctive antagonisms are not easily mastered even if your authorities tell you not to give in to them.

Putting others first may be a morally "good thing," but what about that sneaking feeling that it would be nice if someone, sometime, put you first instead?

Where you have difficulty in asking for equality, never

mind prioritizing yourself, being outer-directed can be unnecessarily life-limiting. If you do manage to act on your own wishes, you may feel so guilty that you spoil the experience for yourself.

BEING INNER-DIRECTED

Some people are much more inclined to turn inward to their own sense of self for direction. It can almost seem as though this kind of person doesn't need any external confirmation, so confident are they in their own judgment, so clear about what they want or what they need to do. They don't seem to be directed by others, only by an internally generated sense of value and purpose. I once heard a colleague describing another as "ruthless," just because she had said at the beginning of a meeting that she had to keep strictly to time because of her child-care arrangements and had then insisted on keeping the discussion really focused and purposeful. She was certainly being inner-directed!

Explorers, visionaries, entrepreneurs and inventors can all be inner-directed. Inner-directed people can be extroverts or introverts. Social behavior is not the deciding factor—it's more that they are driven or motivated by something internal rather than by the influence or opinions of others.

You might be outgoing in the way you relate to other people, or you could just as easily be a quiet and self-contained person.

Advantages

You will rarely find decision-making difficult, because you instinctively know what you want or need to do. Even when you are debating the merits of several possible options, since you are debating both with and within yourself, it's primarily yourself that you have to satisfy. This can apply both to your sense of life purpose and to the pleasures, treats and indulgences life holds out to you.

You may enjoy a feeling of independence, or perhaps see yourself as a free spirit. You are likely to enjoy breaking new ground, being innovative, and not needing to rely on others to tell you what to do. You don't need other people's opinions to ratify your chosen actions, and you probably enjoy working alone.

Disadvantages

Being clear about what you believe and want doesn't automatically mean that other people will accept your ideas or approve of your actions. In fact, they might consider you opinionated or selfish. This can happen even when you are working toward a goal that isn't self-serving. What gives you the right to determine how things should be done? Even where others do agree with something you propose, your timing may not dovetail with theirs and they may feel rushed, bullied or not listened to. Because of this, in family or organizational life you could find yourself out on a limb, committed but without the support you might need in order to carry your ideas forward.

Being a loner can sometimes feel lonely. Not needing to work with others can sometimes make you feel isolated. If you do have to work in a team, you may feel like a square peg in a round hole.

WHAT'S YOUR DEFAULT SETTING?

How do these descriptions fit you? Maybe you are a teenager, caught between the values you learned at home and at school and finding your own value for things. Maybe you have established a career and are now wondering if its values are worth devoting the rest of your working life to. Perhaps you have been made redundant at some time, or seen your last child leave home. You have probably decided more or less which end of the meta-program spectrum you naturally belong on. One way to explore this further is by monitoring the discussions (even arguments) you have inside your head. NLP calls these your "internal dialogue."

> **Internal dialogue** The inner conversations we hold. These can involve different parts of ourselves in discussion/conflict with each other, as well as conversations between ourselves and our significant others. The content can involve both replayed and imagined exchanges.

Internal dialogue can be hugely influential, precisely because we are so often unaware of it. It is another filter that sits between us and what we think of as "reality"; yet, in the very process of filtering reality it is also acting to shape that reality, because it causes or reinforces feelings, clarifies lines of argument and prompts certain actions rather than others. Internal dialogue happens all the time and, once we learn to monitor it, it can also help us understand where our sense of direction is coming from. Internal dialogue, in other words, is something that everyone experiences.

Our internal dialogue is "transparent" to us in much the same way as a personal computer: we are usually unaware of its workings while it's occurring—and often even afterward, too.

If our internal dialogue is based on the assumption that things are hard, or difficult, or require qualities we don't have, this will help set up the way we manage our lives. If it is based on an outer-directed reliance on procedures and on other people, we will find it difficult, if not impossible, to act in a self-reliant way. If it is based on an inner-directed sense of purpose and mission, we may find ourselves dreaming up new methods or solving problems—or running into opposition that we hadn't expected or prepared for.

What kind of things are being said inside your head—and whose voice is saying them? Is your internal dialogue populated by a "cast of thousands" from your life, both past and present? When you do stop to pay attention, you can sometimes catch the very tone of a remembered voice, talking in phrases you may have heard over and over until they have became part of your own "script." Is that voice supporting you in an inner-directed or an outer-directed approach to life? Is its support relevant, or helpful, in your actual circumstances?

There is an interesting and useful concept in NLP: that language conveys not only the immediate, obvious messages but also the "meta-messages"—messages that simultaneously tell us something over and beyond the face-value content of what is being said—and this is particularly true of internal dialogue.

> **Meta-message** This is a message that goes beyond the face value of the actual words spoken, offering either a metaphorical commentary on them or a message at some higher or deeper level (going beyond the words).

The meta-message of my therapy teacher's mantra "think on your feet" is that even in the heat of the moment when you may not have time to think logically, you can trust your instincts to tell you what's right. You don't need to "know" intellectually; you don't need to follow a script; you can safely and appropriately improvise. As such, this can be an extremely empowering message for an internally directed person to receive, especially when they are not floored by pressure. Someone who is externally directed, on the other hand, might find it alarming and disempowering, as I now realize. This kind of person is more likely to be thinking something like: *How on earth can I do the right thing unless I know beforehand what it is?*

Much of the internal dialogue we engage in can carry influential meta-messages. One of my clients, hesitant and lacking confidence for most of his adult life, eventually remembered his father's repeated saying, "Never volunteer." The reticence his father had found useful as a conscript in the army (where volunteering can mean additional or more dangerous work) had carried the disabling meta-message to his son that to take any initiative would be to put himself at risk. Because the message was operating at a higher (meta) level, my client wasn't aware of its effects, even though he remembered the actual words. Is your internal dialogue broadcasting meta-messages to you? What are their effects?

To bring your internal dialogue into greater awareness, here are a number of questions you can ask yourself.

1. Whose voices am I receiving on my interior frequencies?

2. What are the meta-messages I am getting from others, and are they enabling or limiting me?

3. Are these messages even relevant to me and my life now?

4. How do I recognize the voice that is truly my own?

5. How influential are other people's voices as opposed to my own?

6. How much of my internal dialogue is taken up with what should or should not be done?

7. How much involves argument or conflict?

8. How much is enabling, freeing or creative?

9. How much is self-critical?

10. How much is self-encouraging?

11. What light do my answers throw upon the extent to which I am outer- or inner-directed?

THE BEST OF BOTH WORLDS

NLP sets out to help us have more choices than we started with, so the contrasting columns below start with how your default setting is likely to be operating and then shows you how you can extend or add to your range.

If you are outer-directed	If you are inner-directed
You realize others see things differently from you. **Now** consult yourself more and give more weight to your priorities.	You often don't stop to wonder how others see things. **Now** imagine yourself in their shoes.
Remind yourself that others' views are not more or less true than your own.	When people react to what you say or do, **ask yourself** what this tells you about how you are coming across to them.
When your head says "yes," check out whether your body agrees too.	When you want to go ahead with something, ask yourself if there is anything else you need to take into account.

Knowing how things stand between you and the rest of the world allows you to be more flexible and to make more informed choices.

In assessing the relative weighting you could give to different viewpoints, you are not seeking some kind of mythical "balance" between them. What you are looking for is what kind of relationship between inner- and outer-directedness is appropriate or useful in the circumstances. You are not seeking a compromise, either; "compromise" all too often means losing out somewhere.

Only by establishing some kind of relationship between internal and external sources of direction can you function effectively in the world. Operating from either extreme is liable to cause a breakdown in communications, or in effectiveness. This brings up the notion of cost. If you are inner-directed, adhering to your "mission" will have its costs to those around you, even if that mission is an altruistic one. Whether you are a prophet, a CEO or an inspirational teacher, following your path is likely to have costs in terms of personal relationships, physical exhaustion, worldly goods or the time to enjoy them. If, on the other hand, you are outer-directed, adhering to your path will have different costs. Career progression, recreational time, personal space, self-care and self-maintenance can all be compromised, sacrificed or curtailed in the name of moral imperatives or others' needs.

There is always a cost to how we operate. By becoming aware of our default setting on the inner/outer-directed continuum we gain the opportunity to assess the costs both to ourselves and others in relation to the benefits. Perhaps even more important, we open up the possibility of maneuvering along that continuum in relation to the nature and demands of the situation itself.

BRAIN-BUILDING EXERCISES

EXERCISE 1 *Stop, look and listen*

When children are being taught how to cross the road safely, they are often told to stop, look and listen. This simple rule of thumb can help save us from the pitfalls of our inner- or

➤

outer-directedness. It reminds us to look out for danger—in this case, the dangers that are part of the way we naturally go about things. Inner-directed people run the risk of leaping before they look. Outer-directed people are inclined to say yes without wondering if they should be saying no (or perhaps, "I would prefer"). The simplest way to start building your inner–outer flexibility is to build in a momentary pause before you act or open your mouth! This is especially true when what you are about to do is to agree, disagree or offer your opinion. Pause before you commit yourself.

1. Take a breath—literally. It takes a few seconds, giving you precious time to think.

2. Remind yourself of your default setting and how it's likely to be directing you.

3. Imagine briefly how you would act or what you'd say if you were coming from the opposite end of the spectrum. What would happen then?

4. You may well find that you now have a somewhat different idea about what to do. If you are not sure, give yourself even more time to think. If someone else is involved, for example, you may need to say that you want more time to think before giving them your decision or opinion.

EXERCISE 2 *Finding your mentors*

If you are outer-directed, you are quite likely to have identified your most important mentors already. You may, however, be unduly influenced by them at times, or be in

➤

danger of operating on rules and precepts that are now past their use-by date. People whose parents lived through the Depression and the Second World War, for example, will probably have taken on board their parents' frugal make-do-and-mend way of life and their anxieties about the future. They may be limiting themselves by acting accordingly even during times of expansion and affluence. Now that the financial climate has changed again, expansionist views and values that once seemed appropriate will need re-examining. Check out how appropriate and how relevant your mentors are to your situation and needs now.

If you are inner-directed and unaware of being significantly influenced by others, you may actually be missing out on support or inspiration that could be helpful to you. When you are under pressure or have decisions to make, internal mentors can support you, advise you and save you from the kind of mistakes you are prone to making. How can something that is just an idea in your head achieve so much? When we internalize a person or an organization, we take on board not just what they actually did or said but what they stand for. This means that we have some sense of how they would react, and what they would advise even in a new or unforeseen situation. We extrapolate from the known to the unknown.

Some years ago a colleague and I were about to attend a meeting where we knew we would have some tricky negotiating to do. As I walked to catch my train, I asked myself who I would like to have with me in that meeting: whose skills and whose presence would carry me through most effectively? One of the people who "accompanied" me was my NLP trainer, a skilled strategist and inspirational leader. Another was my father—even though he had been dead for

➤

many years, his belief in me was (and is) a cornerstone of my self-belief. The third was my young daughter who, even then, always encouraged me in what I did. Not surprisingly, my colleague and I were successful in our negotiations!

1. What kind of support or advice would help you in making your decision or acting effectively?

2. Who do you know, or know of, who exemplifies the information or the personal qualities you need? The "knowledge" doesn't have to be firsthand. A historical figure or a character from literature can be just as effective a mentor as someone real and known to you. The "reality" and the "knowing" are both in your mind!

3. Take a little while to call up this person in your mind as fully and as richly as you can. You may find that as you do so you begin to get a sense of how they would see the situation you are in, and how they would act. Don't feel disappointed if you don't get a clear idea immediately. You are just as likely to feel their support and benefit from their guidance moment by moment as you go through the situation itself.

EXERCISE 3 *Consulting yourself*

In this exercise you will be trusting and growing your body's wisdom. Whether you are inner- or outer-directed in terms of values, you can call on another very important source of information to check the appropriateness of your responses and your ideas. That is the language of your body. I call this "your somatic wisdom" because your "gut feelings" and immediate

➤

muscular reactions to things are not filtered through your conscious processing. You do not "decide" to frown when puzzled or when you disapprove of something—it just happens. You do not decide to itch or stretch when you are bored any more than you decide to yawn or allow your eyelids to droop. These are the physical manifestations of what is going on inside you, whether or not you are aware of them.

If you are outer-directed, learning to monitor the language of your body is a great way to tap into a different kind of knowledge, one that can give you a useful counterbalance to the precepts you have internalized from outside yourself. Somatic (body language) responses are usually immediate, and if they run counter to what you think you should be doing or feeling, you can take it that going ahead without further exploration may mean problems later on.

1. Before you say yes or no, check how your body reacts to what is being proposed. Are you physically comfortable? Or do you feel a bit more tense, or irritable, angry or sad? What are your responses telling you?

2. If you are inner-directed, other people's somatic responses will help provide you with valuable information, counterbalancing your limitations and helping you to better anticipate the effects your words and actions might have.

3. When you are speaking in a meeting or in conversation, watch the other people involved. What are their expressions saying? Are they still, or moving? What kind of stillness? What kind of movement? If you are not sure, tell them what you see, and check what it means as far as they are concerned: "You are looking puzzled. Would you like me to run through that again?" or "You are frowning. Does that mean you're not happy with my suggestion?"

HOW THEY DO IT

Nikki Green, teacher

66 I get so much pleasure out of helping others to learn. I have a really clear sense of what principles and values underlie what I'm teaching, and how my subject's roots go back into the past; yet I know that every individual I teach has to experience for themselves what this can mean for them and how the subject can enrich their lives. My satisfaction is in helping them find a way to do that. Teaching fulfills and enriches myself, yet at the same time it's utterly self-less. 99

CHAPTER **8**

What Drives You?

Motivation is energy, and energy is always directional. It can be directed at avoiding what isn't wanted or at moving toward what is desired. The potential power of both types of motivation is the same—it's just that the energy involved propels in opposite directions.

BEING MOTIVATED "AWAY-FROM" vs. "TOWARD"

What makes us act? Some actions are aimed at avoiding unpleasant consequences, such as being told off, being found out, feeling pain, getting on the wrong side of the law or the tax man, having a penurious old age, and so on. Others are aimed at achieving goals and goodies: a bigger house, a better job, an interesting life, a comfortable retirement, recognition, or a satisfying partnership. At first sight, you'd think everyone would want to avoid the things on the first list, and everyone would want to aim for the things on the second list. But in real life that's not what happens. Some people put their energy into avoidance before satisfaction (in fact, they derive satisfaction from successful avoidance), whereas others focus on what attracts them, even to the exclusion of some of its possible pitfalls. These are the extremes of a meta-program that helps guide our actions "away-from" or "toward."

Which way shall we go?

Decisions help create the kind of future you prefer—in fact, decisions build a relationship between you and your future. Understanding what drives your decision-making can be the beginning of making that relationship more effective and more life-enhancing.

Some things will attract most people. Some things will repel the majority of others. But decision-making is even more complex than that: it's as if different individuals generally feel one or the other kind of force more strongly, almost regardless of what's actually involved.

Subtle, or not so subtle, persuasion

Advertisers, the persuaders par excellence, know how motivation works. Whenever you open a magazine or catalogue, someone will be trying to influence the decisions you make by weighting the way they present information to you. Here are two examples:

"Your time, your story . . . Tell it your way." (Pulsar watches)
toward

"Combats the 7 visible signs of aging." (Olay)
away-from

Advertisers aim to get you aligned with their product, so that the decision to buy it seems natural and appropriate. How do they do this? Not just by drawing your attention to the merits of their products but by slanting their presentation so that they take account of the way in which you make decisions.

If you take a quick look at the advertisements in a news-paper, magazine or catalogue you will quickly realize that some sophisticated advertisements don't just try to latch onto one kind of motivation but make sure they cover all readers by offering a hook for both kinds:

"We say no to letting hard surfaces damage your back. And yes to footwear that protects it." (MBT, The anti-shoe)

"How 'going green' can save you money . . ."
(*Verdict* magazine)

"Double your money in-store now" (Tesco)

As you read these, were you more strongly aware of the attractors—protecting your back, saving money, getting more for your money—or the repellers: risk of damaging your back, danger of global warming, increasing cost of living? When you see advertisements, which approach is most likely to prompt you to buy?

Looking more closely

It's really important that we don't fall into the trap of thinking that toward is automatically better because it's positive, or that away-from is automatically negative and life-denying. The words "positive" and "negative" cloud the issue because they have acquired a judgmental loading. The terms "away-from" and "toward" don't have such judgmental loading, and instead make us consider the real issues: what's appropri-ate, what's helpful, and what are the consequences of the way our energy tends to be directed. Positive is only right in the correct circumstances, because it can also give rein to hasty decisions, unwise impulses and words that should never have been spoken. On the other hand, negative can save us from ourselves, from the law, from unwise decisions and from fatal accidents. There is no inherent value-loading on either of them!

As a coach, I have worked with many self-employed professionals. All need to keep financial records, and both kinds of motivation can get them doing so: an away-from motivation may alert someone to the possibilities of tax investigation (better keep accurate records, then), while a toward motivation may emphasize that proper record-keeping is part of being a good professional.

BEING TOWARD (MOTIVATED BY ATTRACTION)

Toward people are honeybees: they enjoy seeking out the good things (good to them, that is). Every day can have its exciting moments. Looking forward is one of the key characteristics of a toward person. Even quite small things can offer their quota of promise. If you have a toward motivation and are an in-time person (see Chapter 5) you are likely to be drawn to immediate delights and rewards. If you are a through-time person, a toward motivation may help you undertake longer-term projects and achieve goals further into the future.

Advantages

Life can be exciting quite a lot of the time, because you automatically scan for interest, pleasure and stimulus. Every day has its potential quota of things to look forward to: "What shall I have for lunch?" can be as pleasurable a choice in its own way as deciding to meet a friend, book a theater ticket, get details of a potential job or find out more about a house or car you might want to buy.

You can frequently enjoy a sense of achievement. Anything you want and then get, however small, can potentially bring you much satisfaction.

Things that are new and different seem very vivid, because they promise to make life better. You are always looking out for improvements and refinements. This doesn't necessarily mean you are dissatisfied, only that you operate on a basic belief that better things are still out there. When you think you may have found them, you get a charge of excitement. Task-completion can be quite easy if you want to do something, because before you even begin you will be imagining your satisfaction at the time when it's completed: this "compelling future" can act as a powerful incentive both to start a project and to see it through.

Compelling futures This is an NLP term for something so vividly and realistically imagined in the present that it sucks you inexorably toward making it happen in the future. Compelling futures can be positive, as in the case of people who have a dream and then work to realize it, or negative, as with those whose fear that something will happen actually contributes toward bringing it about.

We can create compelling futures deliberately by imagining our goal or dream in realistic detail, engaging each of our senses (vision, hearing, physical and emotional experiencing, smell and taste) to heighten its attractiveness. If we want to make something seem less attractive, we can "dumb down" its most compelling sensory elements; for example, picturing it in black and white instead of color, picturing it smaller or less distinct, adding a disapproving voice-over, etc. If we want to make a negative anticipation less compelling, we can alter the elements of our imagining in a similar way to play down the realism of the idea so that it becomes less engaging and less inevitable.

Disadvantages

What is on your horizon can seem more attractive than what's already present. Being mentally ahead of yourself like this can mean that you overlook or undervalue what's happening now. You may miss out on the full richness of your present experience and you could also overlook early indicators of difficulties or problems that could be averted by prompt action now. At work, looking out for new methods or projects to get your teeth into in the future may mean that you don't complete what you're currently working on. (There is an important overlap here with the meta-program for in-time and through-time. Such overlaps are explored in Chapter 12.)

Having an eye to new gadgets or new possessions that promise improvements to your private life may mean you end up with a cupboard full of relatively little-used kitchen equipment, a garage full of specialized tools that only rarely get to do their stuff, and a wardrobe full of shirts or sweaters, each of which seemed attractive when you saw them in the shop or the catalogue but which are actually barely different from each other.

New doesn't automatically mean better. Exciting prospects may not actually deliver. Your ever-ready enthusiasm may disincline you to ask the searching questions that would test out how far something is really likely to add value to your life before you say yes or reach for your credit card.

You can be unduly influenced by the prospect of pleasure offered by a potential decision, because it will always be more vivid and seem more likely than any associated downsides. This can make it difficult for you to say no—a much needed ability if you are to control the impulse to enjoy yourself in pleasurable activities. At work, the prospect of doing something interesting, or of being valued by your manager or boss, can mean you ignore or override important factors like the workload you have already, the extent to which a piece of additional work is going to be central or peripheral to your concerns, and so on.

BEING AWAY-FROM (MOTIVATED BY AVOIDANCE)

Away-from people are like shy, wild creatures, most at ease when things are smooth, harmonious, legal and safe. Your sharp eye for potential risk, danger and difficulty means that you can often avoid them breaking through into the calm, managed life you enjoy and thrive in. Watching out for potential difficulties keeps you in a state of alertness, ready to respond at a moment's notice. You are most comfortable when you know you have protected yourself against what you fear happening. (There is a whole profession based on this: it's called insurance.)

Advantages

Away-from reactions are akin to the basic flight/fight mechanism, which gets animals (including humans) away from danger in the shortest possible time. For this reason, away-from responses are to be respected, in others and in yourself.

If you have an away-from motivation and are in-time, your short-term avoidance decisions will help you make life easier or simpler. If you take a through-time view, away-from estimates about the future can help you avoid difficulties further ahead. Because you spend a lot of your time anticipating what might go wrong and planning to ensure it doesn't, you don't usually get caught unprepared. This makes you a valuable—often essential—contributor to the efficiency and smooth running of the groups, teams, organizations and families you belong to.

Disadvantages

You can be so busy looking out for difficulties that you can lose out on good or enjoyable things. When someone gives you feedback, you will want to use it to help you avoid criticism or mistakes in the future, rather than to help you maintain or enhance what you are doing well.

Being alert for the negative things that could happen tends to increase the amount of anxiety and pressure you experience. You have probably gotten so used to living in a mildly anxious state that you don't even notice it. You may even feel strange or uncomfortable when good things happen: "Have I forgotten something?"

Away-from people don't easily relax, because lapses in vigilance can mean making mistakes or being unprepared for what they fear. They may not "hear" compliments because they don't feel as "real" or important to them.

If you are away-from you can find you are checking and rechecking. At times, you may not even find it easy to trust yourself! (Did I remember to turn the gas off? Did I say everything I meant to say?) You are governed by "mights" and "might nots," which feel more real and more likely because you spend so much time thinking about them. You may spend time and energy avoiding things "just in case." You may reject new and unknown things simply because their outcomes are unpredictable and therefore to be feared.

Avoidance of pressure or discomfort in the short term may actually cause problems for you later on. Telling white lies, making excuses, or not speaking your mind when you disagree with something or someone, are all examples of away-from behavior that can sometimes backfire.

WHAT'S YOUR DEFAULT SETTING?

A good question to ask yourself when you are faced with a decision is: "Am I more focused on delivery or deliverance?" In other words, am I switched on by what something offers or promises to deliver to me, or is my attention taken up in finding ways to be delivered from its possible impact? Try running this question in relation to a range of decisions you make: decisions about holidays, purchases, friendships, children, hobbies, and so on. You are likely to get a clear idea of your essential motivation pretty quickly!

Listen to the language you use when you're talking about decisions or risks. It's likely that your speech will give you away, even if it's just you talking to yourself. Words like "avoid," "prevent," "don't want," "make sure X doesn't" all reflect an away-from motivation.

Where you find you are responding in a way that runs against your usual pattern, get curious about what this exception tells you. Everyone's decisions will be influenced by their habitual degree of toward or away-from motivation; but they will also be influenced by which part of the brain is processing any one particular choice. Recent research on the neurology of the brain, summarized in Jonah Lehrer's book *The Decisive Moment*, made use of MRI scanning to show exactly which parts became more active in processing certain kinds of decisions. Decisions can be processed by parts of the brain that access feeling, or alternatively by others that access rationality. Both kinds of processing are important, and each can help or hinder us in making wise decisions.

There isn't a correlation between the parts of the brain that do the processing and whether a person tends to be toward or away-from in their motivation. Rather, the nature of the brain area doing the processing lends it a different kind of coloring or flavor. Decisions processed by the emotion-rich areas of the brain will have an emotional quality to them.

The excitement, fear, wanting, dreading, anxiety or euphoria that you might be experiencing tell you that your emotional processing has been at work, regardless of which kind of emotion you are feeling. Decisions processed by the rational part of the brain will feel more low-key, and you will be aware of your reasoning working away to help you assess factors and probabilities.

THE BEST OF BOTH WORLDS

Knowing whether your motivation is naturally away-from or toward is really useful both at home and at work. Recognizing the signs in other people allows you to understand them and work with them more harmoniously. In groups and teams, an awareness of each type of motivation can help you function better, taking account of everyone's built-in bias so that you are able to make more thoughtful decisions on the basis of feelings, reason, aims and evidence. Attempting to overrule opinions that are based on the opposite way of seeing simply doesn't work, because it doesn't take account of what drives the feelings and the judgments involved. Only when people feel that their viewpoint has been understood and respected will they be prepared to make any concessions or compromises.

If your motivation is toward

Your attractions drive you. **Pause** before you act on them. Things that are worth having will usually keep. Reflecting before you act helps minimize both mistakes and guilt.

If your motivation is away-from

You are quick to spot risks and dangers. **When you feel wary**, try to identify what is really involved and how likely it is that what you fear will actually happen.

If your motivation is toward	If your motivation is away-from
Your emotional brain tells you at once when you like something. **Engage your reasoning** as a reality check—it will either back up your instinctive response or help you detach from it.	Once you have spotted a potential danger, your emotions rush in and make it seem very real—and therefore likely. **Engage your reasoning**. Let it provide ammunition to support your instinctive flight/fight response or to help you "feel the fear and do it anyway."*
When something attracts you, you focus on it alone. **Broaden your focus** before you act. Ask yourself, "Have I got one of those already?" and "What happened last time I did/said that?"	The more you go over what you fear the more likely it seems. **Do a reality check** by asking yourself how things actually turned out last time you felt like this.
Attraction loads your imaginings in favor of successful outcomes. **In your head**, run through future scenarios to get a more balanced view: how might your decision turn out? What could be its unintended (systemic) consequences?	You are pretty quick to take evasive action, but the first strategy that occurs to you might not be the best. **In your head**, run through future scenarios where you act slightly differently each time. What kind of effect is each of your decisions or responses likely to have?

* From the book of the same name by Susan Jeffers.

BRAIN-BUILDING EXERCISES

EXERCISE 1 *Delivery and deliverance*

1. Think of a decision you have recently made. Was it aimed at delivery or deliverance? Jot down some of the factors that seemed important to you at the time.

2. Now change the wording you have used so that you turn delivery language into deliverance language or vice versa. Here are some examples:

Toward (delivery) *becomes* **away-from (deliverance)**
I wanted a more comfortable sofa ➤
I wanted to be less uncomfortable

I took the public speaking course to boost my confidence
in making presentations ➤
*I took the course in order to be less nervous and
embarrassed speaking in public*

Away-from (deliverance) *becomes* **toward (delivery)**
A complex project like this can easily go wrong ➤
*Complex projects are more challenging and could deliver
more exciting outcomes*

I rejected the promotion, because I hate having to
manage other people ➤
*I rejected it because being a team member brings out
more of my talents than managing does*

I hate change and disruption ➤
I thrive when my life is calm and managed

➤

3. Read out your examples and notice carefully what changes you feel as you move between one version and the other.

4. If the contrasting format makes you feel uncomfortable, ask yourself exactly what it is about it that has this effect. How could you help yourself feel more comfortable taking a different stance from your usual one? In what circumstances could this be useful to you?

EXERCISE 2 *The other person's shoes*

1. Think of someone whose motivation contrasts with yours.

2. Think of an occasion in which you disagreed about a decision that you were both involved in making.

3. Place two chairs opposite each other (or two pieces of paper, one with your name on it and one with theirs). Sit in "your" place and remind yourself of what you thought and why.

4. Now move to the other person's space. What did they say at the time? How did they stand and look? As far as you can, adopt their body language and say aloud what they said. What other thoughts come into your mind about what it was like for them in that situation?

5. Move back into your space, face the imagined other person, and let them know (either aloud or silently in

➤

your mind) that you understand and respect their viewpoint and their feelings. Using what you have learned in the previous steps and in Exercise 1, try to present your views in a way that will make sense to them within their frame of reference.

6. Whenever a discussion about decision-making has gone wrong, use this pattern as a way of debriefing yourself and helping you to understand just where each party failed to communicate effectively with the other.

EXERCISE 3 *Choreographing the future*

1. Think of a decision that has to be made in the near future which involves yourself and people with a motivation that contrasts with yours.

2. Using designated chairs or spaces, check out your viewpoint and then that of the others involved.

3. Rehearse in your mind how you will show them you respect their viewpoint and help them to understand where you are coming from.

4. Then go one step further, and make your case for what you want to happen but within their terms.

5. Use this strategy to help you prepare for any upcoming discussions involving people with a different motivational drive.

HOW THEY DO IT

Robert P., shop owner

66 I have two very different attitudes toward money. I save for my pension and make sensible investments so that I'll never end up living in a cardboard box, like people in Africa where I grew up. But I also invest some money in exciting—even risky—things, because I enjoy the thrill and hope they'll work out. Knowing I've covered the away-from possibilities means I can enjoy being toward. 99

CHAPTER **9**

What Grabs Your Attention?

Two kinds of "alert buttons" help us to scan incoming information so that we can determine its significance. Something catches our attention either because it resembles things we already know (it is similar) or because it doesn't (it is different). Similarities and differences describe the relationship between things. The ability to notice and remember patterns is hard-wired into living creatures and can be essential for their survival. It can also help them thrive.

> 66 We might say that 'knowing' is a state in which useful patterns in the world have been registered, and can be used to guide future action. 'Learning' is the activity whereby these patterns are detected. 99
>
> GUY CLAXTON, *Hare Brain, Tortoise Mind*, p. 18

NOTICING SIMILARITIES vs. DIFFERENCES

In my first teaching job, at Sussex University, I was partnered to run a series of interdisciplinary seminars with an experienced colleague, John. One day, after our seminar, John and I were chatting over coffee. "Wasn't it interesting," John said, "that when we were talking about [such-and-such] all the women got really involved and all the guys fell silent?"

"Fascinating," I said. Actually, I hadn't noticed, and I realized that this was John's respectful way of introducing me to a skill he felt I needed, and that has been invaluable to me ever since: noticing patterns in everyday behavior and working with their implications. It has made all the teaching, therapy and coaching that I have done over the years subtler, more astute and more relevant. My training in literature had actually got me noticing linguistic patterns before that day at Sussex: I just hadn't recognized it at the time. As Caroline Spurgeon said in her groundbreaking book on Shakespeare's imagery:

> The imagery [a poet] instinctively uses is . . . a revelation, largely unconscious, given at a moment of heightened feeling, of the furniture of his mind, the channels of his thought, the qualities of things, the objects and incidents he observes and remembers, and perhaps most significant of all, those which he does not observe or remember.
>
> *Shakespeare's Imagery and What It Tells Us*, p. 4

Our language patterns reflect our unconscious thinking. Noticing them allows us to follow what's going on beneath a person's actions and what they say. It was noticed that the characteristic metaphors of Margaret Thatcher's speeches, for example, were often about conflict, even when she was not actually talking about it! The combativeness that came through in her words gave away how she experienced the world and provided anyone who recognized it with a vital clue about how to work with her, or around her, more effectively.

The ability to notice both similarities and differences is essential for development and survival. If something has changed from what we're used to, at the least we will have to adapt, but we might have to take evasive action or protect ourselves.

- Differences can be exciting, as with new ideas, new experiences and new possessions. Any of these, of course, can also be experienced as threatening.

- Similarities feel safe. Things that don't change don't require us to adapt, and the absence of change can feel reassuring. Similarities in ideas or behavior can also be confirming, because they allow us to respond on the basis of what we already know and to predict the future with some confidence.

- On the other hand, when nothing changes it can be boring.

BEING ATTUNED TO SIMILAR

You notice patterns and may easily make links between things that are similar in one way even if they are quite different in others. You probably delight in anything that involves variations on established patterning. Jazz, fashion, literature and cooking could all bring out your sense of delight in "themes and variations." You can easily recognize and apply ideas, whether they involve actual or virtual (mental or interpersonal) components!

It's possible that being attuned to similarity may make you more comfortable fitting in with others than standing out against them, but this depends on whether you use similarity as a mental sorting device or as a more extensive life habit. You could be a very individual, non-conformist person and still have similarity as your filter of choice.

One client of mine belonged to a very stable work team and found that its predictability began to get him down. One day in a typical team meeting he found himself paying attention not to the content of the discussion but to its process. He began to list the things that seemed to occur every time. By the end of the meeting he hadn't taken in anything that had been discussed, but he did have a list of 12 "Rules for Team Meetings" which, rather like the rules you get with board games, he knew could summarize for any outsider what it meant to "play" in this particular team. In sheer exasperation, he printed off his list and took it to the next team meeting. "I'd like us to think about how we behave and whether being so predictable really works for us or limits us," he said. A very lively discussion followed—and people began to identify just how the stability of their relationships and their patterns helped and hindered them at work. My client took a big risk in confronting his colleagues like this, so it's not a pattern to recommend as such. However, picking up on a key habit of an individual or group and pointing it out to them very neutrally (not judgmentally) can often get them appreciating patterns that work or beginning to question ones that are less effective.

Advantages

Learning is a process based on pattern recognition. Once you have noticed something repeating (for example, that $2 + 2 = 4$, or that the sound of pots and pans in the kitchen means dinner will soon be on the table) you register it as a pattern. Now, you expect it to occur again, and being able to predict the future successfully in small things makes you feel secure and more in control. Having the comfort of security and control releases energy for managing things you can't predict.

Being able to recognize a range of commonly occurring patterns helps you identify others that are broadly like them, and so you are able to extend your range of coping or managing: for example, social skills you learned in childhood can be applied in more complex situations as you grow up, enabling you to feel more confident when meeting strangers.

As someone who spots similarities, you have the potential ability to bring ideas together in innovative ways, or to apply skills or tools developed for one field to help solve problems in another. You are likely to register social, business or personal "trends" emerging and be in a position to work with them or make the most of them.

Disadvantages

If you prefer what you know and are anxious about what you don't, you may restrict your exploration and thus limit what you can learn and achieve.

Staying within the comfort zone of what is familiar can deprive you of the enrichment, advancement and fulfillment that new information, new learning and new situations could bring you.

Colleagues may see you as uncooperative or as blocking change out of sheer cussedness. When a venue manager in a recent television documentary was invited to attend a meeting of all the staff, managers and consultants seeking to improve the venue's services, he responded simply and aggressively, "I don't do meetings." This kind of attitude in someone powerful can block progress entirely. In someone less powerful it can cause others so much frustration or irritation that the person gets left out, sidelined or creatively dismissed.

BEING ATTUNED TO DIFFERENT

The dance of detection starts with observation and moves rapidly on to curiosity: it shifts from noticing that something doesn't fit to asking why. This is the essence of being attuned to different: first you notice and then you ask the questions. The differences that you notice aren't just the "bad" or "suspicious" ones, of course. Things also stand out because they are new, exciting, outstanding, original, life-enhancing, joyful, amusing, and so on. Even in terms of basic survival, good things need to be noticed: the best grass, the safest cave, the most attractive mate . . . If you are someone who naturally registers differences, you will probably move on to a third step: creating theories about any differences and seeking evidence to test them.

> 66'Built noticin'—improved by practice,' said Lord Peter quietly. 'Anythin' wrong leaves a kind of impression on the eye; brain trots along afterward with the warnin'.'99
>
> DOROTHY SAYERS, "The Vindictive Story of the Footsteps That Ran," in *Lord Peter Views the Body*, p. 148

As far as your inner world and your sense of self are concerned, you might take difference as a personal life stance, choosing to avoid seeming like everyone else, or you might just rely on difference as a criterion for mental sorting.

Advantages

You will easily spot the one figure on the spreadsheet that doesn't fit. You will notice the smallest signs of change in someone's mood or behavior, which could alert you to help, support or defend yourself against them. You might make a good accountant, therapist, bouncer or police officer.

If you naturally notice differences, you will probably develop a good eye for distinguishing what is truly new and original. In other words, you will probably have what it takes to become a good critic, evaluator or trainer.

If you combine different with away-from (see Chapter 8), you may be a key defensive player in your family or organization, because you will move very rapidly from noticing something that doesn't fit to taking evasive action. You won't miss the subtle indicators of impending personal or professional disasters, but you will act on the first small signs where other people might wait for more evidence—waiting until it is too late!

Disadvantages

This very same rapid reactivity may make you become defensive or take flight even when you don't really need to. Although prey animals do save their lives by flight, they often run away "just in case." This can make life more stressful than it needs to be.

Differences are more noticeable than similarities, but similarities occur more often. If you are struck by differences, you can miss a lot of potentially useful, even important, information that builds up in slow-drip fashion as people's words and behavior give their thinking and their essential natures away.

WHAT'S YOUR DEFAULT SETTING?

Here are some questions to help you work out whether you are more attracted by similarities or by differences. If you find that your answers fall fairly evenly into both categories, look through them to see what other sorting patterns may be operating; for example, you might be attracted by patterns of similarities in your home and work life but enjoy having differences as a "spice up" in holidays or leisure activities, such as reading and hobbies.

Similar	Different
If you could afford it, would you prefer to keep up with the trends in fashion?	Would you rather stand out and be a trendsetter?
When you go to a restaurant, do you automatically choose what you had the last time because you enjoyed it so much?	Do you choose something you haven't had before?
When you have found an item of clothing you like, or an author you enjoy, do you look out for more of the same?	Do you enjoy buying clothes from a variety of shops or discovering new authors to read?
Have you always driven the same make of car?	Do you regularly look through catalogues for new gadgets?
Do you still have friends from when you were at primary school?	Do you enjoy making new acquaintances?
Have you always stayed in one career, or perhaps worked for the same employer?	Have you shifted between different jobs and professions?
Do you hate moving house?	Do you enjoy moving house?
Do you usually prefer to visit the same place for your holiday each year?	Do you enjoy visiting different places on holiday?
Are you happy to do the same leisure pursuits you have for many years?	Do you enjoy learning new skills and hobbies?

THE BEST OF BOTH WORLDS

As long ago as 1970, Alvin Toffler (the American writer who virtually created the concept of investigating the future) remarked in his book *Future Shock* that some people positively relished "stimulus hunger" (newness and change) and seemed remarkably tolerant of disruption in their lives. He went on:

> Close analysis of such people often reveals the existence of what might be called "stability zones" in their lives— certain enduring relationships that are carefully maintained despite all other kinds of changes.
>
> *Future Shock*, p. 342

Such areas of stability, Toffler noted, included remaining for years in the same job, having long-term marriages and friendships, and maintaining the same daily personal habits. Any one of these might act as a personal "buffer" that helped the person absorb change and disruption.

Translated into meta-program terms, this suggests that if we can learn to offset our natural preference for similar or difference with its opposite we can not only enjoy the advantages of both, strategically applied, but also better equip ourselves to manage a world that is changing exponentially. Toffler's examples make it clear that individual solutions are both personal and infinitely adjustable. Someone whose private life is very stable could allow themselves more latitude in exploring difference and novelty at work or in their leisure pursuits. One client I had was someone with a strong similar preference both at home (he was in his forties and still lived with his parents) and at work (he had worked for the same employer for 20 years). Yet he relished extreme sports and adventure holidays. These expressed and contained his need for things that were different. It is easy to imagine some-one for whom the reverse could be the case.

Spice it up

Training yourself to become more alert to both similarities and differences allows you to get a closer match between any situation and what you need from it.

Do you need energy for something challenging?
(**different**) ➤

Can you free some energy by developing or relying on your routines (**similar**)?

Are you content enough with things as they are (**similar**) but just a bit frustrated? ➤

Can you find an activity, a holiday, a book, a friend that will from time to time add edge and stimulus to your life (**different**) and make you relish the security and comfort of what you know even more?

Curiously enough, these spice-it-up suggestions all rely on adjusting the combination of similar and different that you have in your life. That's because differences that are not dangerous are usually life-enhancing, even when they consist of bringing some routine or order (similar) into a life that is predominantly based on change and variety (difference)!

This could be summed up as: if what you are used to doing (or being) isn't working for you, do something different.

If you register similarities	If you register differences
Remind yourself that doing the same thing again goes round again, but not forward. It's the essence of boredom—and security!	**Remind yourself** that difference is at the heart of danger as well as development. Also remind yourself that it's the essence of what's outstanding!
When you hesitate about trying something new, **remind yourself** that if you like it, it could become a new favorite!	Look carefully at your life and its patterns. List all the similars you take for granted, and **remind yourself** that doing some things the same releases energy to experiment with things that are different.
Practice looking out for small signs of difference (weak signals) in established patterns. These will help alert you to potential disruptions and opportunities before they become established, and so increase your power to choose and control.	**Remind yourself** that every difference stands out from something. What is the pattern (similarity) that you have registered being broken?

BRAIN-BUILDING EXERCISES

EXERCISE 1 *Weekly workout*

If you prefer similar, set yourself a challenge to take one familiar thing each week and make a slight variation to it; for example, if you prepare food and drink for breakfast in the same sequence, change that sequence one morning. For one meal, eat your fruit or sweet before your savory. What do you notice as a result of bringing something you usually

➤

do automatically into awareness like this? Continue with this stretch, taking a different pattern or habit each week, and escalate the order of difficulty. How long do you think it would take you before you felt able to offer a compliment to a total stranger?

If you prefer difference, choose something small in your life that you could make routine or habitual. Some "difference" people have few routine patterns—you may be one of them. Maybe you could routinize your getting-up or going-to-bed activities, doing the essential tasks in more or less the same order. The challenge is not just doing it but learning to cherish its very routineness. Even if you already have a more-or-less routine pattern, take time to consider and appreciate what that patterning gives you. The chances are that it helps you feel a sense of appropriateness or completeness, because routines don't just get things done, they also mark something out. Morning and evening routines can become domestic rituals that help you celebrate the beginning of a new day or appreciate and reflect on the passing of one that's just closing down. An alternative version of this challenge is to notice and celebrate some other pattern that is already routine but which you normally ignore or think of as dull or boring. If you stop to look, what might be the virtues of this hitherto overlooked pattern?

EXERCISE 2 *Life class*

1. Try thinking of someone whose position on this metaprogram contrasts strongly with your own. If you know them well, ask them how they would experience some of the following:

➤

- An unexpected phone call or visit from someone who hasn't been in contact with them for a while.

- A change in arrangements or in a plan initiated by someone else.

- A social invitation from an acquaintance.

- Being asked to take on a new responsibility at work.

- Being asked to mentor someone who has just joined your organization.

- Having an unexpected windfall of money to decide what to do with (for example, a tax rebate, proceeds of the sale of a personal possession, a small inheritance.

If you don't feel you can have this kind of conversation with them, use what you know of them from past observation to imagine how they would feel, think and behave in some of these situations.

2. What can you learn from such a different way of experiencing? Is there anything you can "borrow" straight away from this person's way of being to enrich or stretch your own? If you feel uncomfortable about stretching yourself in this way, ask yourself just what feelings, fears or risks are making you feel like this.

Recognizing the patterns we take for granted is the first step toward driving them rather than being driven by them. Only when we bring into our consciousness something that has been taken for granted (in other words, unconsciously organized) can we begin to modify, enrich, develop or change it. So the disruption of the understanding we had before (even if what we had was total ignorance of a subject) is actually the essential basis for any learning; in other words, only by breaking patterns can we go on to build both understanding and skill. By noticing our own patterning we can begin to break free of its potential tyranny and ask ourselves the enabling question, "What's most appropriate here?"

HOW THEY DO IT

Frances Massey, university administrator

❝ I suppose my default is to notice similarities. I know I compare things all the time—books, pictures, plants—all the things I like. I also know I get to understand new ideas or plans by starting off with the familiar aspects of them. But—and it is a big 'but'—the whole point of noticing similarities always seems to be that it provides the basis for defining difference. When I was teaching in higher education I used to tell students preparing assignments to choose "compare and contrast" topics whenever they could; and then to start by identifying all the similarities between whatever they were comparing, so as to establish the baseline. Then I would ask them to go to what I thought of as the most interesting part, which was to define and describe all the differences! I have retired now, but recently my niece, who was starting an Open University degree in law, telephoned to ask for advice about how to write an essay in which she had to compare and contrast two kinds of court procedures. When I told her to start with the similarities and then move on to the differences, and what she thought about them, all became clear for her. She got a great grade!

➤

For 25 years my husband and I, plus members of our family, have had a holiday every year in St. Ives in Cornwall. We go to new places most years too, but the whole point about St. Ives is that we know and love it so well, and are so interested in the art that has been produced there that as soon as we arrive we can get straight into what is new! It makes for very special holidays."

CHAPTER **10**

Are You a Task-Person or a People-Person?

If you were asked, would you think of yourself as a task-person, who's more concerned with getting on with the work in hand than forming relationships with others? Or are you a people-person, who values the relationships you have with others, even in the workplace? The answer you give reflects how you value each of these possibilities in your mind—and so it will have an important influence on the choices you make and the actions you take out there in the "real" world.

> 66 Alpha leaders understand human instincts, and spend a good deal of time creating coalitions of people who are willing to work together to make exciting things happen. 99
>
> ANNE DEERING, ROBERT DILTS AND JULIAN RUSSELL,
> *Alpha Leadership*, p. 15

The authors of the book quoted above are implying that both are important, and that good leaders aren't inherently either task-people or people-people. What they are really good at is marrying the two together.

I was once asked to coach a promising young woman in a large company: I was told that she was excellent—even outstanding—at her work but very poor at personal relations. In fact, there had recently been a formal complaint against her on these grounds. My brief was to help her improve her interpersonal sensitivity and skill so that she could continue to move up the career ladder in accordance with her technical ability. One day we were discussing small everyday ways in which she might nurture a greater connection with her staff: asking them how their weekend had gone was one example. "Do I have to do it even if I don't care about the answer?" she asked sadly. This instinctive response confirmed what she and I already recognized: she was a task-person. It was greatly to her credit that over the time we worked together she made real efforts to understand how other people felt and experienced things and to adjust her management style accordingly.

Another person I coached in the same organization managed a team that included both internal staff and external contractors. She generated loyalty and also efficiency. Her staff turnover was low, conflict was infrequent and promptly resolved when it did occur, and the work got done to a high standard. But she said, "I do wish my manager wouldn't keep referring to me as a people-person. It comes across as so soft and dismissive—as though I'm warm, vague and woolly."

DISTINCTIONS THAT CAUSE DIVISIONS

The idea that someone is either a task-person or a people-person is both crude and divisive, yet it's used very commonly in workplaces. As with many ideas in common currency, the fact that it's accepted as a valid distinction goes a long way to making it become real. Reality for any one individual is the sense they make of what's happening: reality for organizations is what the organization collectively understands to be the case. So big firms have workers (task-people), human resources staff (people-people) and managers who may be either or, with luck, a bit of both. Lip service may be paid to the importance of people skills for techies and of efficiency for those with a natural preference for working with people, but everyone knows who's really which.

Most people are not just one or the other, of course. Engineers have friends and families and can put themselves wholeheartedly into the "softer" roles these involve. Mothers, nurses and social workers set targets, manage workflows and evaluate performance. Is such a simplistic and permeable kind of distinction at all helpful then? As with the other metaprogram distinctions, I think it can be, because like any either/or option, it makes us reflect on where we place our own emphasis. Whatever our words say, when it comes to actions are we voting for the job or for the people? And when we act, what kind of baby may we be in danger of throwing out with the bathwater?

BEING A TASK-PERSON

You will naturally find yourself being drawn to ask what has to be done or what needs to be done. You will be happiest when there are clear answers to these questions, when your own role is well defined and when emotions are not complicating the situation. Once you know what needs doing, you will usually feel energetic, even driven, until it's been accomplished. Task-people can be great at clarifying situations and at marshaling resources to manage them. They aren't unaware of personal stuff, but for them "personal is not the same as important."

Advantages

If you are a task-person you will have clarity and focus about what the job is and getting it done. Values like application, conscientiousness, reliability and the importance of standards tend to underlie a task-person's approach, and all of these help them become clear about what's involved in something before they even start. Questions like "What's involved?" and "How will we measure/assess . . . ?" can be invaluable in setting up projects both at work and at home.

You meet targets and don't get distracted. You feel very connected to the projects and goals that you take on, and the strength of the connection gives you fuel to drive toward accomplishment and completion.

You are able to set personal feelings aside, not be swayed by personalities. You don't get caught up in interpersonal issues—this can be refreshing and clarifying.

Disadvantages

You may ignore important feelings or interpersonal under-currents, thus offending others and/or impeding the task itself. Believing that this dimension isn't relevant doesn't make it go away. A task-person's limitation can show up in underestimating its importance or in recognizing it but not knowing what to do about it.

Task-people can be accused of "railroading" others: their resentment at this may mean they ignore or even isolate you.

You might miss out on a rich dimension of work life (no gossip, limited discussions and/or confidences). Work has as much of a social dimension as social life, but task-people can miss out on more than just information: fun, amusement, caring and sharing can all pass them by.

You may seem rather inaccessible, so others don't speak up until there's a real difficulty. This can be a problem when it comes to receiving (or giving) the subtle signals that alert us to both issues and opportunities. The ability to pick up such signals depends on both the number of connections in someone's network and their receptivity.

> 66 Everyone can hear a shout, but only those with exceptional sensory systems can hear the barely audible whispers where most of the opportunities and timely warnings lie. 99
>
> DEERING, DILTS AND RUSSELL, *Alpha Leadership*, p. 104

A task-person may come across as uncaring. If you make it clear, however unconsciously, that it's the task you prioritize, people will feel that in slighting their feelings you are slighting them. Even when they know they are overreacting they will still feel you haven't understood them adequately.

You might oversimplify, and can underestimate difficulties that can be caused by people's feelings or by their interrelationships. Any task that involves people implies managing people as part of the task! You may find you get frustrated when "people stuff" hampers something getting done. Frustration, of course, is a feeling, which task-people may prompt in themselves just as much as in others.

As a task-person you may find multitasking difficult, because you prefer to have a clear sense of a single overall priority, and multitasking invariably involves juggling multiple factors, such as attention, priorities and time.

BEING A PEOPLE-PERSON

You enjoy interacting with others, and can derive pleasure from strategizing and managing the complexities of relationships both at home and at work. Confusion and subtlety engage you more than simplicity, because it's the nuances of thought and feeling that make people unique, and it's that uniqueness that you relish. You enjoy puzzling over motivation and meaning, seeking what lies under the surface. You understand that voice tone and body language say as much as spoken words or deliberate actions, and you factor them into your thinking and theorizing.

Advantages

A people-person builds good connections and enjoys having meaningful friendships. You create a pleasant atmosphere and you're nice to be around—cultivating harmony and believing this is as important in work groups as in domestic and social situations.

People-people genuinely do believe others matter, and this message comes across convincingly from you. Most people respond well to this message, so people-people may generate more commitment and more energy in those around them, thus creating "virtuous circles":

Feeling you matter ➤

you show more commitment ➤

you get more positive responses ➤

which in turn confirms the feeling that you matter ➤

and so on

> **Virtuous circle** (opposite to a vicious circle) A situation in which something good elicits a good response, leading to further sequences of alternating beneficial actions and responses.

A people-person will often be patient because they seek to understand where others are coming from. It's not the same as thinking the best of others, just that you make the effort to understand how they experience things. This empathic understanding may form the basis for intelligent strategizing that results in increased cooperation, better task performance, and so on.

Disadvantages

You may get distracted from the task, especially if it involves putting pressure on others. People-people sometimes tend to shy away from concepts like "confrontation," "pressure," "being direct" and "target-setting" because these are associated with a fear of being experienced as demanding or unsympathetic.

You may find it hard to give or receive feedback, especially if it involves negative judgments. Most people are not trained in giving feedback in a way that is free of emotional overtones. Many find it difficult to receive either praise or criticism without discomfort and embarrassment. This makes for mutual discomfort and often for an inappropriate and sometimes dysfunctional delay in feedback being passed on.

If you prioritize people skills, you may fail to recognize the value of task skills. People-people can sometimes be dismissive of others who are talented at getting things done.

You may equate being assertive with being aggressive. People-people are usually good at imaginatively stepping into others' shoes, which may also mean that they find it difficult to express, let alone stand up for, their own feelings, needs and beliefs, seeing this as being selfish.

You may find that you fudge boundaries through reluctance to appear dominant or aggressive. Your fear of being thought bossy, difficult, hostile or demanding by others may result in softening off the messages you give to them, so that distinctions, boundaries and requests all become blurred and unclear. Opting for harmony in the short term can cause problems and misunderstandings in the longer term.

Taking different perceptual positions Being in **first position** means experiencing things from one's own perspective; taking **second position** involves imagining oneself in someone else's shoes in order to appreciate their view of a situation; taking **third position** involves observing a situation as if detached, even when this means observing and evaluating oneself.

You may take things personally when a situation doesn't really require it, and so cause yourself and others unnecessary grief. You may also find it hard to say no, so that you take on too much. Being thought of as "nice" can make a people-person overaccommodating, especially with others who aren't shy of making their wishes clear or asking others to do things for them. The default response of a people-person may be to say yes, but often this means regretting the impulse and then having to either back off later or put up with the burden that they have colluded in taking on.

People-people can be too patient or too empathic, and may not recognize when others need confronting, stretching or prodding to take steps that will actually help them forward. When people-people take on positions of authority (such as parents or managers) their generosity toward others and their wish to understand them and spare unpleasant feelings can blind them to the value of clarity, boundaries and firmness in testing, stretching and provoking those others toward further development. How can someone "step up to the plate" if the plate is not presented as being a degree beyond where they are at the moment? How can they discover deeper resourcefulness and realize greater potential in themselves unless something calls it forth?

As a people-person you may find you lose track of important task-related needs such as targets and time frames. (This can be an area of overlap with being in-time rather, than through-time. For meta-program overlaps and clusterings, see Chapter 12.)

WHAT'S YOUR DEFAULT SETTING?

Task-person	People-person
Do you feel comfortable when you know what needs doing and know you can do it?	Do you enjoy speculating about why people do what they do, or ask yourself how they are likely to feel and react?
Do you feel less comfortable, or impatient, when you realize that other people's feelings may be involved?	Do you go over in your mind situations that have occurred in order to understand them better, and rehearse ones that may occur in the future in order to test out different strategies for managing them?
Are you sometimes surprised by the way someone reacted to you?	Do you enjoy listening to other people talking about themselves?
Do you tend to use phrases like "what it all boils down to" or "what needs to happen is . . ."?	Do you try to avoid being disliked?
Do you feel at a loss, in your private or work life, when someone else is upset or angry?	Do you sometimes feel that your identity has somehow disappeared from the picture because you have omitted to take yourself into account?

THE BEST OF BOTH WORLDS

If you are a task-person	If you are a people-person
Remind yourself that dealing with feelings is not irrelevant to doing the task but often a necessary part of it.	**Remember** that tasks involving people are still tasks.
Allow more time for a task than your first estimate—people eat up time!	**Watch out** lest your people focus may sometimes blur your purpose and lessen your energy or commitment.
When things don't go as you expect, **talk** them over with a people-person to discover what you are missing.	**Cultivate** a friend or colleague with a task focus to help you keep on track.

BRAIN-BUILDING EXERCISES

EXERCISE 1 *The all-rounder*

When you are thinking about something that's going to happen in the future, the way you anticipate it is likely to be colored—and therefore shaped—by whether you are processing it primarily in task or people terms. This exercise is designed to help you develop a more all-round way of managing. You might find it helpful to do it in an open space where you can move to each of three physically distinct approaches. Designate each beforehand in your mind. Use a labeled piece of paper on the floor in each position if this assists you in changing your perceptual position.

1. In first position, ask yourself how you naturally anticipate this situation evolving.

➤

2. Move to a different position, which on this occasion is that of someone with a contrasting default setting. How might you see things if you were them?

3. Take a different position again—the "view from the bridge," in which you can see everything and everyone involved. How does the situation seem from this position?

4. Now get close to your original default position, standing just to one side, or slightly behind it, without stepping right back into it again. What new information do you now have to add to what you started with? How might this change things for you when the situation you are thinking about actually happens in real life?

5. Finally, step back into your first position again, taking all this new information with you. Allow yourself a few minutes (with your eyes closed, if that helps) to assimilate what you have learned.

Only rarely in life can any of us safely act according to one kind of priority alone. Most situations, whether domestic, social or work related, involve managing some kind of balance between people and task priorities.

HOW THEY DO IT

A. M. Frances, senior university manager and strategic planner

66 By instinct I am a people-person. I am very motherly. I am, I think, very aware of people's reactions to what I say. It made me a good teacher because I could always see what

➤

the students were thinking, and I knew how to engage them with what I wanted to discuss. When I suddenly became a senior manager I thought at first that the same way of going about things would be fine—that I would still be in the business of discussing things and getting people to understand what I wanted them to understand. But I soon realized that that was not it at all. Colleagues have their own ideas and do not often expect to have to learn new ones!

A senior colleague said to me, 'Never go into a meeting without knowing what you want to get out of it.' That was excellent advice. I learned to have a plan, and to use my sensitivities to be quick-footed about carrying it out. I also learned that it is sometimes very short-sighted indeed to be too concerned about people's feelings now if tomorrow they will lose out. **"**

CHAPTER **11**

Are You a Thinker or a Doer?

"To do is to be." SOCRATES

"To be is to do." SARTRE

Of all the meta-program distinctions, the apparent opposition between thinking and doing appears to be the most artificial. The ability to think is an essential part and parcel of being human. Yet everyone thinks and everyone does: the issue is whether you like to think about your doing—and indeed about your thinking!—or whether you prefer to think of yourself as a "doer," letting your thought processes largely take care of themselves at an unconscious level.

To my mind, this meta-program is primarily a filter for what kinds of mental activity you choose to allow into your awareness rather than one for what activities you engage in.

It's almost as though each of us feels most at home either in the touchable, seeable, feelable realm of the external senses or in the ethereal realm of abstract ideas, speculations, hypotheses and conclusions. Both realms, of course, are equally real—and equally unreal—because in both cases information is mediated through a processing intelligence that makes the meanings that we end up with. Are you more comfortable being surrounded by concrete actuality or by the subtle and unseeable miasmas of the mind?

As I write this, I'm looking at the screen of my computer. I can create, change and rearrange the words I use and monitor these processes on-screen. I can do clever things like creating tables and boxes. I can play with fonts and type sizes. I can even take delight in being able to manipulate these features. What I can't see and don't know about is what's going on off-screen, although everything that's visible to me is in fact dependent on it. This is a simplistic analogy for our mental processes: some are visible whereas other equally essential ones are not.

OUR UNCONSCIOUS

We can think, we can even think about thinking itself, but both of these processes take place in consciousness (that is, "on-screen"). Yet there is so much more going on in our brains than this small "visible" amount. Quite apart from the organization, monitoring and continuous adjustment of everyday physiological processes (digestion, homeostasis, circulation, and so on), much of the information we depend on for conscious thought is organized, stored, marshaled and retrieved from unconscious "holding." What we think of as learning is dependent on the process of transferring information that was first acquired and organized consciously into areas of "unconscious competence" where the learning mechanisms and pathways are forgotten. Once stored unconsciously, the learning is available when needed but we no longer need to think about how we acquired it or what's involved in using it.

If we look at thinking and doing in this way, perhaps it's more accurate to say that people who categorize themselves as "doers" may think they are using their muscle memories but are, in fact, relying equally on their unconscious mental processes—and they are doing so both naturally and contentedly.

> **Muscle memory** is unconsciously stored sequences or patterns of physical actions. Picking up a mug that turns out to be empty when you thought it was full (or vice versa) clearly demonstrates how we unconsciously estimate the amount of pressure and power we think an action will require. The error in estimating is what brings the action into awareness. When we get the estimate right we just pick up the mug! Complex routines such as those involved in everyday actions as well as specific applications in sporting or artistic fields all rely on the acquisition, elaboration and progressive refinement of muscle memories.

BEING A THINKER

As a thinker, you will enjoy reflection and analysis, and be stimulated by solving problems through mental maneuvering. You will be comfortable with theorizing, speculating, accumulating and testing evidence. You can easily move ideas around on the screen of your intelligence—rather like exploring a building through computer graphics. Thinkers may relish uncertainty, because it invites them to engage with it in a way that certainty does not.

Advantages

If you think before you act, your actions are more considered so less prone to the kind of error that comes with off-the-cuff behavior. If you think after you have done something, whether or not you thought about it first and whether or not it turned out well, you have more chance of learning from your experience.

Thinkers can easily envisage different pathways and outcomes, which is useful for planning successful strategies. If you are a flexible thinker you will find it relatively easy to put yourself into different perceptual positions where you can assess situations in a more rounded and complex way, thus taking account of a fuller range of factors, before acting or making judgments.

Disadvantages

As a thinker you may sometimes cultivate inward absorption to the point where you find practicalities difficult or irritating. This is often largely a question of prioritizing rather than of an actual inability to manage in the practical world, but it may lead others to think of you as impractical or airy-fairy.

You may switch off to others, and this can easily be misinterpreted as a lack of interest. You may underestimate the importance, and significance, of actions (both your own and those of other people). You may sometimes get bogged down in complex ideas or nuances.

BEING A DOER

You like to think of yourself as hands-on and "straightforward" rather than complex. You take pride in being direct rather than abstruse in your communication. You may actively dislike complexity and complications, and perhaps consider them unnecessary. Doers are usually outward-facing, and when they do think about themselves they don't take pleasure in navel-gazing. They are happiest maneuvering things, not ideas: their subtlety and complexity is primarily kinesthetic.

They may sometimes fear thinking and thinkers, rather as an inexperienced swimmer might be apprehensive about deep water.

> **Kinesthetic** Feeling-based (both physical and emotional). Kinesthetic information is a key sensory system used to receive information from outside and process it inwardly. It includes both physical (somatic) information and emotional information—the latter belongs under the same heading because, as we have already seen, emotions involve physical expression and physical changes.

Advantages

Other people might find you restful because they sense that you are not devious. You are usually good at solving practical problems, and may have either procedural or inventive skills. As a doer you may not be troubled by emotional baggage or undercurrents. You probably get on with things without too much reflection or hesitation.

Disadvantages

You can lack self-awareness, and may be unaware of thoughts and feelings that are important to other people. You may underestimate your own intelligence and may also be underestimated by others, especially within the education system. You may have found "academic" subjects difficult at school, or felt disadvantaged and undervalued by comparison with peers who had a more abstract cast of mind.

You may get frustrated when you are unable to "do something about" things that trouble you, or be inclined to jump in with practical solutions to other people's emotional problems when what they really want is a sympathetic listening ear.

WHAT'S YOUR DEFAULT SETTING?

Doer	Thinker
Given a choice, would you prefer to do something physical?	Would you prefer something that involved sitting and thinking?
When you have a problem to solve, is your first impulse to "do something"?*	Are you more likely to "get your head around the problem"?*
Do issues like conceptual puzzles make you feel more helpless?	Do issues like practical breakdowns make you feel more helpless?

* Everyday phrases can often be highly telling. Which are you most likely to use here?

1. At the end of a day that felt like a really good one, what sorts of things would you have been engaged in?

2. Quickly think of three things you're proud of having accomplished. Were they thinker things or doer things?

THE BEST OF BOTH WORLDS

I began this section by implying that we are all thinkers, whether we like to label ourselves that way or not. There's a Latin aphorism that goes: "Nothing is in the understanding that was not earlier in the senses" (*Nihil est in intellectu quod non prius fuerit in sensu*). The early investigations from which NLP developed uncovered just how true this is: when different people use the word "thinking" they will probably assume they are talking about the same activity as someone else who uses that word, but this isn't the case. What we are all doing when we "think" actually varies from person to person, because each of us is combining the different elements of thinking into a very personal mix. Thinking involves imagining to ourselves, so there's individual variety in how we do this. But there's even more opportunity for variance, because each of us relies more or less on different kinds of sensory information to do our "thinking" with. Each of our senses is like a system in itself, because it processes certain kinds of information rather than others, and so NLP calls them representational systems.

> **Representational systems** The sensory processes (seeing, hearing, touching, smelling and tasting—referred to in NLP by the more technical terms: visual, auditory, kinesthetic, olfactory and gustatory) through which we mentally manage information. This includes not only information that reaches us directly from outside via our senses but also information internally stored and generated in our minds.

Each of us can call on every kind of sensory information to do our thinking, but in practice we each have our own favorites. Some people's "thinking" takes the form of mental picture-making and film-viewing. Some people's experience is primarily kinesthetic: it's as live and real in their minds as in their external experience. Others exist in a rich world of sound: voices, conversations, both real and imagined, as well as music and natural sounds. To a lesser extent, smell and taste also play a part in our mental existence.

Once we are aware how sense-based our thinking is, the distinction between "thinkers" and "doers" becomes even slimmer. Doers have to think in order to act, even if they choose to avoid certain kinds of introspective, speculative or analytical thought, if possible. Thinkers have to rely on their senses to populate their internal worlds with richness and meaning. However we label ourselves, we all have to make use of our minds to control our bodies, and we all use sense-based information as the essential currency of our mental activities.

This subtle overlap was one of the rich areas explored by the American sports coach Timothy Gallwey. Working at much the same time as the NLP developers, he became fascinated by the extent to which people's minds affected something as apparently physical as playing tennis or golf. He thought of it in terms of a dialogue within the person between "the conscious ego-mind" and "the body and unconscious computer-like mind":

> When a player comes to recognize, for instance, that learning to concentrate may be more valuable to him than a backhand, he shifts from being primarily a player of the outer game to being a player of the inner game. Then, instead of learning concentration to improve his tennis, he practices tennis to improve his concentration.
>
> *The Inner Game of Tennis*, p. 114

Getting the best of both is about training oneself to ask some apparently simple but actually very stretching questions. As a first check on yourself, when you are either reflecting or about to act, ask yourself, "What's missing?"

In other words, invite yourself to "round out" the way you naturally understand the situation, the task or the problem. What's missing will be the kind of information that could be provided by the way of processing that's less obvious, or less comfortable, to you.

BRAIN-BUILDING EXERCISES

Coaching makes use of many apparently simple questions to help people take a different view of situations and to find important information they already have without knowing that they have it. This in itself can be a way of helping both doers and thinkers to access material that's held out of conscious awareness and that cannot therefore be deliberately factored into their understanding or their planning. The majority of these questions can provide you with opportunities for stretching and strengthening the way you manage yourself and your interaction with the world. Appropriately phrased, they can give you powerful leverage for understanding and changing in both domestic and work contexts. You can ask them of yourself in the privacy of your own head, and you can also ask them of others out loud. They are powerful because they are search questions: the hearer has to go inside their head in order to answer them. Search questions not only draw out otherwise inaccessible information, but encourage, tease and sometimes compel the hearer to make connections between thinking and doing.

EXERCISE 1 *Finding out what's going on*

Q: How come? A question for assessing the state of play

This question invites you to speculate about causes and sequences: how did we get here (rather than there)?

Thinkers

You may find this a natural question to ask, but, even so, really engaging with it can prompt you to wonder about "the road not taken." **How else** might things have turned out, and what is the possible learning in that?

Doers

You're likely to look first for outward actions and events. In your case the stretch provided by this question is that it asks you to search for invisible and unprovable things like reasons, motivations, assumptions and processes.

➤

Q: What's really going on? A question that probes below the surface

This is a good question to ask yourself to enrich your understanding of here-and-now situations even while you are actually immersed in them.

Thinkers

Your first response may be to hunt for interpersonal dynamics, symbolisms or undercurrents.
Now look for behavior and language patterns, and for sequences of actions and reactions to ground your suppositions and check your interpretations against external evidence.

Doers

Describing actions and events will come naturally to you.
Now ask yourself what your emotions are telling you. Is this a comfortable situation to be in? Does the body language, voice tone or eye contact between any of the participants give you the feeling of an emotional force field around them? What might that be about? What are your own gut feelings? What might be causing your responses? What do you think might come up next? Have you any supporting evidence for your hunch, and what might it be?

EXERCISE 2 *Approaching things differently*

Q: What else? A question for engaging another way of being

Presupposing that there is more to discover, this is a good question to ask yourself (and others), whether you are a natural thinker or a doer.

Thinkers

Even habitual speculators can settle for less than is actually available. This question prompts you to explore any situation more fully, especially if you remind yourself that the "what else?" also includes what is being done or could be done.

Doers

Few situations are truly simple or direct. This question reminds you to look beyond the surface. In particular, you can use it to help you become more reflective about yourself and more speculative about others.

Q: How else? A question about method

How did you/do you/might you/will you go about something? And what about others' approaches, too? "How?" is a great NLP word. It draws our attention to the fact that there's a method in everything—in thought and action and even, as Hamlet reminds us, "method in my madness." Finding out the method is the first step on the way to having more choice, both about how we do things (both mentally and physically) and where doing them might take us.

➤

Thinkers

You already think about thinking. **How else** might you, or other people, interpret this situation or event? It's also a useful prompt for getting more flexible in your actions. **How else** might you tackle this issue, problem or task?

Doers

How else might you act? And what might be the consequences of that? **How else** might the task be approached? **How else** might the situation be interpreted?

EXERCISE 3 *Context and consequence*

Q: What comes next? A question for identifying possible consequences

This question invites you to frame your here-and-now experience (whether it is primarily reflective or active) in a broader context, as part of a chain of actions and reactions. The question encourages you to see what you are thinking and doing "now" in relation to the possible consequences it can have, within your mind and within the social networks you are part of in your private and working life.

Thinkers

Thinkers are often natural strategists, but the limitation of this is that you may find your mind running off ahead of you. If you are a visionary,

Doers

Doers are highly connected to their experiencing, both here and now, and what they have planned for the future. This question gets you to see

➤

you can sometimes miss out the steps needed to get you from here to there. "What comes next?" gets you thinking about where you could be headed and where you want to be headed—and what will take you there, step by step.

what's happening or what needs to be done here and now in a longer-term context, and encourages you to envisage a number of options before you choose to act.

EXERCISE 4 *Implications*

Q: So what? A question that helps you look deeper for meaning and purpose

When said rudely this question comes across as dismissive. When asked respectfully, as my colleague Jan Pye and I have often done, it can stop you in your tracks, inviting you to step back from what's happening or what's immediately concerning you and to think deeply about its significance and implications.

Thinkers

Thinkers naturally analyze and reflect. When you describe or summarize something, asking yourself, "So what?" encourages you to move from your comfortable mental realm toward the possibilities of action. You

Doers

However comfortable you are about doing, you may be missing out on considering what it's all about: so this was said, and that was done— what does it signify? When you ask yourself (or someone else) the "So what?" question

➤

Thinkers	Doers
have reached an understanding or a summation of how things are: what does it all really add up to? What are the deeper implications and possibilities? Is reflecting enough? Or is there something you actually need to do?	you immediately move into a realm of deeper possibilities and meanings. This larger perspective leads you to re-evaluate. Sometimes it may lead you to discard actions and assumptions that are part of your habitual way of operating. At other times, it may provide you with an understandable rationale for what your gut knew already. In the light of that, you may have ammunition to defend things that seem unimportant, but that in fact have a deeper consequence.

The theme of this chapter has been that doing and thinking are essentially interdependent. Whether you consider yourself primarily a thinker or a doer, you are actually both. The stretch questions ask you to take a step back and examine your own way of being and doing. It's a process that NLP describes as "going meta" to yourself.

Going meta Viewing yourself, or a situation in which you are involved, as if from outside: a God's-eye view, a wider perspective on your own subjective experience; a viewpoint from which you can observe, assess, monitor and even mentor yourself.

If you are a doer, your stretch is in choosing to view yourself as an observer: it's not that different from the way you might learn and refine your practical skills. If you are a thinker, your stretch comes both from thinking about your own thinking and from reviewing how it gets translated into action.

The meta place is an exciting place to be. It can feel restful as well as strenuous, confirming as well as challenging. It's a place where you can engage with every part of yourself.

HOW THEY DO IT

Sandra Shorter, writer and silversmith

66 I have two main roles in my life, and they seem quite contrasting. I write books and articles, so half the time I am playing with ideas. But I also spend time designing and making jewelry. Often when I've been writing for a while I feel I need to become more active, so my 'doer' takes a turn; and sometimes when I'm working with my hands, ideas for my writing occur to me and I jot them down so my 'writer' self can explore them later. It's like a conversation. 99

CHAPTER **12**

How Do Your Meta-Programs Stack Up Together?

Most profiling systems seem neat and tidy—usually too neat and tidy to capture the full complexity of real life! Let's remind ourselves, though, that meta-programming is best seen as a set of guidelines for mapping the extremely complex territory that is you, me and the rest of humankind. It's a system derived from how we are. So when you encounter it, it has a familiarity similar to when you come across your house or street on a map for the first time.

BUILDING PROFILES OF YOURSELF AND OTHERS

Up until now in this book, we have been focusing on one meta-program at a time, but in real-life situations more than one meta-program usually comes into play. And that's not all: each of us may operate from slightly, or even distinctly, different default positions on the same meta-program, depending on different circumstances. Someone who is away-from and procedural at work, like one of my clients, can be toward and inventive on holiday. A crafts-person could be inventive—often linked with being large-chunk—in designing what they make, yet also procedural and small-chunk in actually carrying out their work. Some of the apparent contrasts between meta-program opposites and meta-program likenesses can melt away when people tackle real situations, challenges and tasks.

When beginning to explore your own bundle of meta-program preferences, and thinking about other people's, there are two considerations to bear in mind. First, that there do seem to be some natural affinities between certain meta-programs and, second, that human individuality is so great that you can't safely make assumptions about which defaults will in fact end up bundled together!

YOUR META-PROGRAM PREFERENCES

It's useful to begin by plotting out your natural preferences, based on what struck you as you were reading the accounts earlier in the book.

There are some natural affinities within meta-programs; for example, many people who are procedural are also small-chunk. Some of them may also be away-from. Perhaps you are one of these. A procedural focus can often link with being in-time. Here are some of the natural pairings that seem to occur.

Procedural	Inventive
Small-chunk	Large-chunk
Small-chunk	Toward
In-time	Inventive
Procedural	
Away-from	

And here are some larger affinity groupings that can exist:

Procedural	People-focus
Small-chunk	Outer-directed
In-time	Doer
Outer-directed	Dissociated
Task-focus	
Doer	People-focus
Similar	Inner-directed
	Associated
Toward	
Inventive	Inventive
Through-time	Dissimilar
Inner-directed	Thinker/doer
Task-focus	
Thinker	

The examples probably suffice to show how almost infinite the possible combinations are, and to remind us that we can't be sure that someone who is, for example, inner-directed will necessarily be inventive, any more than someone who is away-from will automatically be outer-directed.

So why bother trying to build a profile at all? First, by paying careful attention we train ourselves to appreciate how a default setting that can at times be a liability in one context can produce marvelous results in another: for example, someone whose sense of detail can drive you (and themselves) mad at times can be the best present-chooser ever—because they find something that really fits you every time.

Second, by thinking about affinities or bundles of meta-programs we remind ourselves of the value of being attentive, asking questions, and appreciating just how amazing we all are in discovering and using the very different ways we can manage ourselves and the world.

Third, this mixture of curiosity and appreciation gives us

the self-confidence to explore the possibility of trying out new ways or attempting a slightly different emphasis from usual. And fourth, when you recognize how amazing and how varied human beings are, it becomes much harder to dismiss someone for a particular attitude or behavior. I think this helps us be more generous while at the same time remaining quite realistic.

As with any information, once you have taken an understanding of the meta-programs on board you can't then unlearn it again. This is true of newly acquired knowledge, but even truer when what you have done is bring knowledge you already had deep in your mind to the surface of your awareness. Once you become aware of what you already knew, you gain more choices. You can now choose how you let the newly available information inform you: you can choose how you work with it; you can choose whether to experiment with it deliberately or whether to let it seep into your unconscious repertoire of tools. Whatever choice you make, the knowledge will not go away.

MANAGING YOUR META-PROGRAM CLUSTER

However your meta-program preferences stack up, the resulting cluster is an important asset that needs managing. At times it can be a great strength, yet at others the very same natural combination can become a liability. The toward–inventive–large-chunk cluster that makes someone a creative problem-solver or artist might also ensure that their finances at best take the form of a pile of receipts in a box—or at worst can only be dredged up from trouser pockets, handbags or car glove compartments—and are still incomplete after much ranting and many headaches. The combination of toward, large-chunk and in-time that can make someone such a fun companion or such a great generator of ideas and projects can, in different circumstances, make them an impulsive spend-thrift with no sense of costs or consequences. The associated, outer-directed outlook that makes someone a good carer for others may at the same time mean that they smoke, eat or drink too much because they don't feel justified in taking time for themselves; or in a domestic setting it may lead to the anxiety or depression that parents (especially non-working mothers) can suddenly feel when their children grow up and leave home.

Take a few minutes to imagine yourself in a particular role: at work, at home, on holiday, for example. Look at your own meta-program clustering in that role, and ask yourself the following questions:

1. What are the strengths of this clustering? For example:
Helps me to . . .
Is useful when . . .
Ensures I avoid . . .
Makes it easier to . . .

- Am I making the most of the resources that I have at home? Or at work?

- How do I know (what tells me?) when I am at my best? What tells me when I am not? (One important indicator may be how you feel—especially what your energy levels are like.)

- What could I do to be at my best even more often and more fully?

- What would I have to change/give up/begin in order to do this?

2. What are the limitations of your characteristic clustering? Take a situation or role—at home or work, or one from both

—where you feel you are sometimes less than effective. Ask yourself the following questions:

- How often is my strengths cluster also a liability?

- Does this tend to happen in some circumstances more than others? (For example, at home; with high-status colleagues; when I'm taken by surprise.)

- What tells me when this is occurring? (Do I recognize it myself, or do I get feedback from others that lets me know?)

- How does it make me feel?

- Could I develop a faster awareness of when this is happening or, better still, of when it is likely to happen? Are there any patterns (similarities) or changes (differences), or any key triggers I could monitor as possible warning signs?

- What might I have to do to minimize the risk of this happening?

- What changes might that involve in my assumptions, thinking or behavior? (For example, many outer-directed people respond reactively and automatically to the perceived values or needs of others; however, saying no or even just taking time to think before responding can create the opportunity for awareness, reflection, and sometimes for responding in a different way.)

You may have found some of the questions harder or easier to answer than others. Take the felt sense of your resistance, fluency or eagerness as additional information. Ask yourself, "What was that about?" (For more about the power of this question, see Chapter 7.)

Now look again at any meta-programs where you have

recognized that you move flexibly between the extremes. Write a brief self-profile to create your own "How I do it" box like the ones at the end of the individual meta-program chapters.

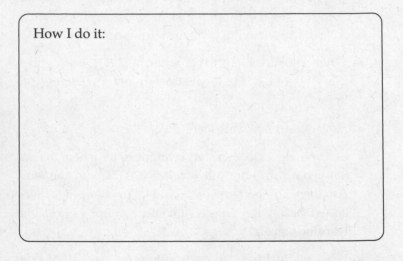

How I do it:

Now jot down what you feel are the key triggers and levers for your personal flexibility. If you are flexible along more than one meta-program axis, check whether your methods for being flexible are the same—which would indicate an underlying pattern—or whether they are different. Can you use any of this information to help you become more flexible on meta-programs where you have a clearer default position?

There's another refinement, too. You may have a specific default in certain situations and a quite different one in others: you are not always inventive, or always small-chunk. The writer Alvin Toffler found that many people who coped brilliantly with change, loved variety and even sought it out (toward, inventive) were able to do so because they resisted change (moved away from disruption) in other areas of their lives, and even deliberately stuck to familiar routines and habits (procedural). By this means they created areas of stability and predictability in their lives, which allowed them freedom to explore and experiment in others.

PROFILING OTHERS

Getting a sense of how other people function is both fascinating and helpful: even a rough idea of their natural clustering of meta-programs helps you relate to them naturally and without friction, so that you can help them be at their best. At the least, it helps you take the pressure off them when they are not at their best, or gives you clues as to why things went wrong. One of my clients, reflecting on someone in his team who didn't seem to be working effectively, suddenly said: "I suppose I should have expected that he would find it difficult to do this. I'm asking him to take a long strategic view (inventive, through-time) but I realize now that he's an in-time detail person. No wonder he's finding it difficult!"

Much of the time, you'll have to rely on observation and pattern spotting for building up profiles of others. To make a start, you could pick someone you interact with frequently and feel you know fairly well, think of a specific situation in which you encounter each other, and begin to collect information on the following:

- **How they approach a task**. Are they methodical and sequential (procedural)? Do they plan ahead (through-time)? Do they just dive in and see what happens (inventive, possibly in-time)?

- **How they manage time**. Do they manage time effectively (through-time) or tend to run out of it (in-time)? Hand gestures may give a clue as to where past and future are located as far as they are concerned.

- **How they manage detail** and how easily they relate the detail of what they're doing to the task as a whole (chunk size).

- **What kind of hobbies or sports** are they are involved with. "Doing" hobbies may indicate someone who prefers to do than to reflect—or, on the other hand, someone who likes to do as a change from thinking.

If someone has a clear "default" on a meta-program, they are probably unlikely to exhibit the opposite behavior with any ease; for example, a completer is probably more likely to respond to away-from reasoning than an idea-generating person (inventive, toward) would.

Also ask yourself, are you recognizing and making full use of the talents of anyone around you who is effortlessly flexible along a particular meta-program?

Building profiles of yourself and others, however tentative the conclusions you reach, can help explain why you feel so at home with some people and so uncomfortable with others. The chances are that you will feel a much greater affinity with people whose meta-programming is close to yours, and less sense of closeness or even comprehension with those whose significant meta-program defaults contrast with yours. Once you have worked out what those affinities and divergencies are, you will be much better placed to understand why someone else thinks and behaves as they do, which is a key step toward building a more (or even more) effective relationship with them.

CHAPTER **13**

How "Modeling" Can Develop Your Flexibility

Understanding the meta-programs, like every discovery in NLP, came through the practice of "modeling." Modeling involves taking something apart to find out what it's made from and how it's put together. We can do this with people's thinking and behavior as well as with physical things like buildings, machines or other created objects. Now it's time to consider modeling in its own right and to show you something of the different ways you can use it to take your flexibility to new levels.

> 66 The objective of the NLP modeling process is not to end up with the one 'right' or 'true' description of a particular person's thinking process, but rather to make an instrumental map that allows us to apply the strategies that we have modeled in some useful way. An 'instrumental map' is one that allows us to act more effectively—the 'accuracy' or 'reality' of the map is less important than its 'usefulness.' 99
>
> ROBERT DILTS, *Modeling with NLP*, p. 30

Modeling helps develop flexibility in two ways. First, we need to model brains that we believe to be flexible, in order to discover more about how they do what they do. And second, brains that are flexible need to keep on modeling "good practice" in order to keep adding to their stretch-and-strength capabilities.

WHY FLEXIBLE BRAINS NEED MODELING

Modeling is not something you tick off and have done with. The more you do it, the better you get at it, the more you learn through it and the more subtle and useful are the discoveries you make. It's the tool that helps you discover more about how things (including meta-programs) work, and at the same time makes you more effective in the way you use them yourself. It's NLP's ultimate multi-tool.

WHAT DOES MODELING INVOLVE?

The word "model" has a number of meanings: (1) something that is the focus of observation (as in a model for life drawing); (2) an abstract concept or set of concepts which outline essential structures and processes (as in a model of social or financial behavior); and (3) the label for a process: the focusing of observation and inquiry in great detail upon a target person in order to find out how they do what they do. The observer/investigator is modeling their subject and seeks to create a map or model of their subject's essential qualities or behaviors. There's a further meaning: when you deliberately set out to offer through your behavior an example upon which others can model themselves, you are (4) "modeling to" them. Like someone "modeling" clothing to potential customers, we can model specific behavior to the people we want to "buy into" it and use it for themselves. Each of these can be powerful and valuable variations of an essential tool you can use to support your brain-building and through which you can apply your increasing meta-program awareness and flexibility.

Getting down to basics

Early on in this book I described how the earliest developers of NLP modeled outstanding therapists. I once heard John Grinder explain how he and his colleague Richard Bandler originally modeled the psychiatrist and pioneer of clinical hypnosis, Milton Erickson. The key to successful modeling, Grinder said, was to take nothing for granted. In working with their own clients, they initially copied everything they had noticed about Erickson: not just his words but his gravelly voice; not just his movements but the awkward posture he had as a result of twice having polio; they even dressed themselves in purple (Erickson's favorite color). Until they had re-created everything about him to the best of their ability, they felt they could not begin to identify and pare away the less significant attributes so that they were left with the "essential" Erickson— the bits that really made all the difference.

Most of us do not have this sophisticated and painstaking level of observational skill, nor do we need it for everyday purposes. Actually, we can use and refine something we have already learned. Modeling is something we have all done from a very early age: we modeled the people who were important to us when we were young. We took every detail about them on board without even knowing we were doing it. That's why we sounded like our parents when we answered the phone—our intonation echoed theirs. That's why children often amuse us by walking just like their mothers or fathers: the copycat stance and action has become part of the child's own way of moving by a kind of natural osmosis.

LEARNING FROM OTHERS

Modeling comes naturally and without any conscious effort to children, and of course it's also a tool we can deliberately use to learn the detailed structures of someone's success. (We can also model ineffective behavior in order not to repeat it.) Provided we can identify enough of the raw ingredients of thinking and action that contribute to someone's style and achievement, we can begin to use for ourselves the formulas that seem so effortless for them. How do we do this? By watching them closely and by asking them questions about what's going on inside their heads. We are seeking to discover how their own particular constellation of meta-program patterning makes them who they are. How does their unique set of defaults—or their easy flexibility—enable them to handle issues or manage life in general the way they do?

If you think about modeling someone you admire, you might find that visual information is your natural way in. Or you might find that it's how the person sounds, the words they use or the speed and pitch of their intonation that really register with you. You might also find yourself replaying and re-creating their body language.

When modeling someone whose meta-programming is different from yours and who is more effective in certain situations because of it, you can observe and model what they say and how they act, and if you are able to ask them about it, how they think.

HOW THEY DID IT

T.D., middle-managing executive

One of my clients found that the impression he made on his work colleagues changed totally when he began to closely

➤

model the behavior, voice tone, pace and body language of senior people whom he really respected. By modeling individuals he valued for their integrity and gravitas, and by changing his own behavior in quite subtle ways to align with theirs, he was able to project his own integrity more effectively, and his ideas were received as if he too possessed gravitas rather than just the intelligence and enthusiasm formerly associated with him. In comparing himself to colleagues he respected for their gravitas, my client realized that he moved and talked faster than they did. One effect was that he made other people—in meetings, for example—feel hassled. He realized that his more senior colleagues felt uncomfortable, so that they labeled his intelligence, confidence and overall "towardsness" as "arrogance." Slowing down his movements and deepening his voice tone helped his colleagues feel he deserved listening to, so that they came to believe his proposals could safely be followed. It was as though what he said now came as the result of considered thinking rather than youthful impetuosity. People—even away-from people—were now much more prepared to listen to him.

Information gathering

What kinds of things might you need to notice, and what kinds of questions might you ask, in order to model someone?

Some things to notice:
- Body language and movement, including whether movement is quick or slow, contained or expressive

➤

- Eye contact and eye movements
- Head and hand gestures
- Stance
- How any particular movements correlate or synchronize with speech
- Any characteristic phrases or metaphors that give away how the person maps the world, and in particular ones that indicate their natural meta-program settings

Some things to ask them:
- How do you manage to . . . ?
- What's going on in your mind when you . . . ?
- What's important to you when you . . . ?
- What do you think the essence of your ability to do this is?
- Are there any particular steps and sequences you follow?
- What assumptions are you making?
- What are you looking for?

Working with contrasts

Modeling depends upon identifying a clear, understandable and repeatable pattern that can be repeated by others. Starting with close observation will usually help you realize just what you need to follow up with questions. Modeling someone whose meta-program defaults contrast with yours is a great way to stretch yourself and to build your flexibility. It's also a great way to help you build a bridge of understanding and rapport, so that you both find it easier to communicate and work with each other.

Procedural and small-chunk people will probably find it easy to ferret out someone's sequences and patterns. But even if you are inventive and large-chunk, you can find ways to get the information you're seeking. When I was doing my NLP training, we were asked to pair up and go for a walk in the park. The partners took turns to lead each other, and the person following had to copy their leader as exactly as possible in order to experience what the walk felt like for the other person. This was a highly inventive and large-chunk task in the way it was framed—one that got us all discovering experiences, processes, sequences and, in short, small-chunk procedures! If you are inventive, what procedures could you dream up to help you model someone you want to learn from or to emulate? The exercise also began by requiring us to act in a similar way to our partner, and through so doing we discovered a great deal about the differences as well as the similarities between us. Watching someone else intently calls for an in-time focus, but considering the implications of what you are seeing and hearing immediately widens your reflection toward a longer time frame. It's a flexibility exercise in itself.

SETTING AN EXAMPLE

Whenever we interact with someone else we are potentially in a position to influence them. By choosing how we behave, we can offer them a "model" of how we would like them to behave. We begin modeling to them. In order to have this subtle effect, we ideally need to have established rapport with them, so that they respect, trust or even look up to us. At the very least, we need to have their attention. Like all interpersonal skills, modeling to others is only really effective if you genuinely believe in what you're modeling and are consistent in the way you do it.

Punctuality is a simple example. If you want your colleagues to be on time for meetings, you are more likely to get them doing so if you consistently model punctuality yourself and if you back this up by starting your own meetings on time rather than waiting for latecomers. The unspoken message is: be on time. It shows respect for the purpose of the meeting and for the other people involved (toward motivation). If you are late you might be considered churlish, or you may even miss something important (away-from motivation). Modeling has a great deal to do with the unspoken, or implied, messages that are being given. An old-fashioned way of describing the process is "do as you would be done by"!

Unintentional influences

Modeling can happen unintentionally as well as intentionally, of course, and so we need to watch out for how our own unconsidered actions might be influencing others at home or work. Over the last few years, television advertising has begun to have some interesting side effects. Presenters of relatively serious programs that have advertisement breaks now tend to begin every section with a mini catch-up for viewers who may have just tuned in. Viewers who started watching at the beginning can find this both irritating and somewhat patronizing, even infantilizing. More serious, however, is that the "catch-up" method is actually modeling passivity to the viewer. They no longer need to bother to remember what has gone before or where the program seemed to be heading. This contrasts sharply with assumptions made by speakers about listeners in previous times. When my father (born in 1903) was a youngster he was expected to listen to an hour-long sermon at church every Sunday and to give an accurate account of its major arguments when he got home. What was being modeled to him through this expectation was that even a child had the concentration span and the memory required to listen attentively, follow an intellectual argument, mark and retain its structure and major headings, and to repeat these articulately some time later.

Changes in social behavior often reflect changes due to modeling that have begun to catch on or become, in a positive sense, "epidemic." When the law was changed to decriminalize homosexuality, for example, it implicitly modeled first a tolerance and then an acceptance of homosexual orientation and relationships. When enough informed individuals began to believe in global warming, the concern and changed behaviors of some key individuals and groups began to model new social norms of concern for the environment on both personal and global levels.

LEARNING FROM YOURSELF

Modeling isn't just about distilling the precious essence of other people! You can also investigate (model) how you yourself do what you do, which will help you identify the central features of your thinking and behavior in given situations that work well or less well for you.

HOW THEY DID IT

S., university applicant

A teenager whom I coached went for an interview and found herself sitting hunched over on the edge of her chair. She instinctively realized—even in the midst of this stressful situation—that this just "wasn't her." In any other context she would have been sitting upright and much more deeply in a chair. So she adjusted her position, and immediately found herself feeling much more at ease and less intimidated by the interviewer. As a result she was able to express herself more fluently and make a much better impression.

➤

This young woman caught herself behaving (and feeling) differently from usual because the difference was so marked, so by modeling the core features of her immediate behavior and contrasting them with her usual behavior she found what she needed to alter to produce a better and more comfortable result. She modeled what wasn't working, modeled what usually did, and adjusted from the one pattern toward the other. She changed her away-from, self-protective positioning to her more usual toward attitude—and with it, changed her feelings too.

We can also self-model to find out our own "recipes for disaster" so that we can begin to change them, "resetting the points" so that we no longer go down familiar rails toward failure, disappointment or missed opportunity. Why does one person always "get dumped"? Why is someone always anxious about new situations even though in the event he manages them well? Why does someone never quite get his business "ahead of the curve"? Why does another do more and more and yet achieve less and less? They might start to find the answers by modeling just how they do that, and just what part their default meta-program settings play.

Building up a picture from layers

Some years ago I wanted to model a great equestrian trainer, Charles de Kunffy, in order to understand how he assessed a horse and rider in a few minutes, coached them through exercises, and by the end of half an hour left them performing so much better than when they began. How did

➤

he do that? Charles hadn't previously thought about exactly how he did this, yet his reply revealed that he used a very complex assessment process. When the horse and rider first came into the arena, he watched how they moved. At the same time, he had in his mind's eye a picture of "how the greats do it": a visual memory of excellent performance against which he projected the here-and-now action he was observing as though overlaying two slides in a projector. This helped him see how his current pupil's performance related to that of "the greats." There was a further element still: Charles created a third and even a fourth layer of mental images, which pictured how this horse and rider would be performing at the end of this lesson, and again how they would be working in six months' time. This elaborate system of visual overlays enabled him to target his teaching very precisely, coaching from today's start to today's finish toward six months' time, all the time in relation to the blueprint of greatness he held in his memory.

Through this complex personal assessment system, Charles was using remembered models, and he was also creating models of possibility. You could try out something similar when involved in assessing performance (either other people's or your own).

Modeling is one of the most exciting, invigorating and rewarding of NLP tools. It's one that links the two halves of this book together. From Part One's exploration of how people filter and respond to information, it helps us move on to consider how we can use that knowledge to become more flexible and more effective in managing the challenging issues of daily life. And that is the subject of Part Two.

NEW WAYS TO APPROACH REAL-LIFE ISSUES

In this part I'm going to help you explore how you can use your newly stretched and strengthened brain in real-life situations. You will see how the meta-programs can be applied in our everyday lives, wherever we may be.

WORK AND HOME

Although work and home might appear to be separate, the choices you face are, in fact, similar: for example, we work with teams at our place of work, but families and friendship networks are teams too. In this part of the book I'm going to treat home and work as contexts that provoke and challenge our skills in essentially similar ways. Thinking of them like this helps us to realize that we do not have to evolve separate strategies for separate contexts.

Each of the following chapters takes a single area of challenge and possibility, identifies the common problems people experience in dealing with it, and pinpoints which meta-programs are most involved. It allows you to realize why some people are good at managing each kind of issue. It also helps you to recognize how your own existing meta-program habits may contribute to your finding that issue more or less difficult to manage, and it shows you how and where you can become more flexible and more strategic.

HOW TO USE THE META-PROGRAMS

Read through the relevant chapter or chapters in Part Two. Before relating the meta-programs to any specific situation, work through the following points:

- Think about your own meta-programs and how they operate. What are your strengths and your liabilities in the situation you are now in?

- If what you're already doing isn't working well, which meta-programs are most involved and how could you become more flexible in working with them?

- If other people are involved in this same situation, what do you know about their meta-program settings and how these would influence the way they approach it?

- What overlaps, contrasts and potential conflicts might exist between you?

- How are you going to manage those, given what you know?

STEPS TO SUCCESS

You can use the following basic structure for problem solving in any aspect of your life:

Step 1: Observe the situation and ask yourself, "What's going on here?" Remember, your assumptions can lead you astray, because they can mean you will be filtering out information you think isn't significant but that could turn out to be important.

Step 2: Reflect on what you have observed. Using the similar vs. different meta-program, look for the elements, patterns and sequences in the situation. When do they apply? Is there ever a time when they don't? What is different at those times?

Step 3: Experiment What changes are you going to make? How should you respond? In your own situation, almost anything you do differently will change the status quo and give you more information. Remember to ask, "How about . . . ?" You don't have to hope you will find the one right solution. Instead ask, "What happens if I do this/or that/or stop doing the other?"

Step 4: Test and evaluate You need to know about the impact of your chosen action, so you need to stop it or vary it and see what happens.

Step 5: Adjust again, if necessary If your first change didn't work, or it didn't have sufficient impact, experiment again.

Here's an example:

Step 1: Observe A mother noticed that her small child tended to be "difficult" on the way home from school.

Step 2: Reflect The mother wondered what was making her daughter cranky every day at this time. Her child was not cranky on non-school days and was happy at school. Was there anything else different on non-school days? Yes—they usually had their lunch at 1:00 pm (school lunch-time is at 12.00), and they often had a drink and a snack at 4:00 pm. Could low blood sugar be causing the irritability? The mother had started by identifying what was similar in the pattern that was causing the problem, and then found some important differences to provide a possible solution.

Step 3: Experiment The next day the mother gave her child a snack to eat on the walk home. There was no crankiness that day.

Step 4: Test and evaluate To test whether her hypothesis was correct, one day she took food but didn't give it at once. Her daughter was grouchy for most of the journey home, so the mother gave her something to eat, and her temper improved within a short while.

Step 5: Adjust again As the child grew older, she was able to tolerate longer intervals between eating, although maintaining her blood sugar level remained an issue even into adult life.

By using these same strategies in various situations, we will continue to learn and benefit from them as we go through our lives.

CHAPTER **14**

Prioritizing Effectively

How do you decide what's most important? How do you decide what to do first—or next? How do you decide whom to please? How do you decide what not to do (or what not to wear)? And what impact can your meta-program patterning have on this? Some people find prioritizing relatively easy, and others find it incredibly hard. But we all have to make choices every day at home and work about what's most important, most valuable or most urgent. All of these choices involve measuring specific possibilities against more enduring or overarching values, principles or goals.

WHAT MATTERS MOST?

Effective prioritizing almost always involves creating a relationship between small-chunk items—for example, tasks to do, actions to take, people to see, allocating your time—and large-chunk items such as goals, values, needs and preferences. Doing this also involves relating specifics to abstracts.

As Steven Covey says:

> If you are an effective manager of your self, your discipline comes from within; it is a function of your independent will. You are a disciple, a follower, of your own deep values and their source. And you have the will, the integrity, to subordinate your feelings, your impulses, your moods to those values.
>
> *The 7 Habits of Highly Effective People*, p. 149

Someone who prefers orderliness (procedural) will prioritize how they apportion their spare time differently as well as having a contrasting approach to a task at work from someone who is inventive. Someone who is outer-directed may prioritize tasks suggested by others or by social or family "tradition" above the possibility of doing something for themselves or on their own initiative.

Only when you have clarified the goals and values involved are you in a position to assess each of your "to-do" or "take-into-account" items adequately. Having your own core standard in mind allows you to assess each item on your (probably overloaded) list against something that is both important and consistent. On a weekend morning you might "need" to do the shopping and washing, and clean the house, so that next week you will have enough to eat and not be living in a mess with no clean clothes to wear. The underlying values are orderliness and taking care of the basics now to make life easier next week. Or, since it's the first fine Saturday for ages, should you grab a picnic lunch and head for the seaside, the country or the local swimming pool? The underlying values here are "making the most of now," sharing pleasure with your partner, family or friends. There is, of course, no right answer—except the one that's right for you and for the situation. Prioritizing helps you become clearer in your mind.

If things need to be orderly for next week to be manageable, you are less likely to resent doing chores while the sun shines; or, alternatively, if you are clear that next week you can put up with a certain amount of chaos or hand-to-mouth survival, you will feel truly lighthearted as you grab your sunscreen and swimsuit.

In deciding what to prioritize you are going to need to bear in mind your in-time–through-time and your toward–away-from preferences, and those of other people who may be involved.

EFFICIENCY OR EFFECTIVENESS?

Prioritizing brings up another pair of interconnected values, too: efficiency and effectiveness. Although they sound alike, they can actually relate to quite different underlying values and have quite different implications. Effectiveness is about the way something is done: it's about economy of effort in relation to outcome, and it's a judgment confined to accomplishing the task itself. It relates quite closely to an in-time perspective, because it's about assessing results in quite a short time frame. Assessing efficiency relates more closely to a through-time take on things: it's about how a specific act or set of acts will affect things, and involves making a future-based judgment about whether the "job done" actually will do the job it is intended to do. Something done efficiently in the short term could still be ineffective in the longer term: for example, if two people at work don't get on with each other, an effective solution might be to allocate them to work on different projects. That way, conflict would be kept to a minimum and a surface harmony maintained. A more efficient approach, however, might be for their manager to spend time with each of them separately and both of them together to help them recognize and deal with their differences.

Most of us probably find prioritizing easier in some circumstances than others. When we are committed to a value, an aim, an action or a person, it often seems easier to make a decision—although this sense of commitment and clarity does not always make for the best choices! Each of us can be helped and hindered by our established meta-program patterning. Knowing its potentialities and limitations can help us feel confident or proceed more cautiously in making the choices we have to make. And when someone else doesn't seem to agree about what is important, reflecting on what we know of their meta-program habits may help us to understand and find a base for discussion and, hopefully, some kind of agreement.

The kind of person who finds it relatively easy to prioritize is likely to have a clear set of values, needs or goals against which to measure possible options, even if these are not fully articulated. Such a person may come across at times as hard, cold or driven or, in contrast, overemotional or reactive, as others find them impervious to pressure, enticement or persuasion. Anyone who is clear about what's important to them may run the risk of railroading others intellectually, emotionally or practically if they don't take time to consider where the others are coming from.

Managing pressure as a team

A common problem at work is what you do when you've got too much to do. Do you try to get it all done? Do you hurry everything and compromise quality in order to meet deadlines? Do you do what you can and blame someone or something else when you don't get it done?

HOW THEY DID IT

HR team in a manufacturing company

This team decided that prioritizing was really everyone's problem, so everyone needed to manage it. They decided to devote 30 minutes of their Monday team meeting to reviewing their priorities for the week, assessing how well they were keeping to targets and deadlines, and deciding what should be done. Sometimes this meant helping each other out; sometimes it meant re-ordering priorities; sometimes it meant asking their manager to make a decision for them. It wasn't always easy for someone to confess they were falling behind, but sharing the information helped them realize that they weren't alone in having to manage pressure and overload. They stopped feeling guilty and frustrated, because they now worked as allies to manage a common dilemma. Even if nothing different could be done, people felt less demoralized, and more able to work with energy and commitment—so sometimes even those tasks that everybody thought couldn't be done actually did get done after all.

Planning for choice

Every kind of choice, of course, relates to some kind of priority. In this chapter I'm going to take you through a number of problem patterns that arise when people are prioritizing, showing which meta-programs are most involved and explaining a key exercise that, with variations, can help you find an effective way of dealing with whichever you happen to be facing. Exercises always take some time, and the temptation is to say, "But I'm in such a hurry/I have so much to do already/How can I possibly spare any more time to do an exercise?" By familiarizing yourself with the patterns at a time when, hopefully, prioritizing isn't so urgent, you will have a strategy in readiness for when it becomes so. Remember, too, that your mind is far, far faster in its ability to flex and react according to a pattern it already understands than your eyes are in making sense of instructions for the first time!

COMMON PITFALLS IN PRIORITIZING

Failing to prioritize at all—instead just starting at the top of the list

You can easily spend a day, a week, a month . . . busily doing what's in front of your nose, interrupting your own work to respond to every call and every query. You probably know the scenario. You won't be surprised to recognize that this is a very in-time response! First, learn to catch yourself at it. Even if you have already done several things like this today, it's not too late to reformat the rest of the day.

Coping strategies:

1. Set up a regular time for prioritizing (or, if you prefer, make time to explore creative ways for channeling your time and energies most effectively) before you feel the need. Use your morning travel time, the time after you have dropped the kids off at school or the first ten minutes at your desk to get today's priorities right, or to reorganize them for tomorrow.

2. If you can, arrange to work at home or in a quiet space at work where you can't easily be interrupted. One of my clients works at home one day a week and doesn't even look at his e-mails. He told me his colleagues were shocked at this, but interestingly enough he didn't get phone calls at home on these days, either, which in itself tends to imply

that his colleagues did recognize a difference between urgency and importance (see more about this on pages 191–2). Sending an e-mail to someone at home comes out of a sense of urgency; not phoning suggests that the senders weren't convinced that the message truly was important.

Assessing things in relation to each other

Which shall I do first? The only way to work this out satisfactorily is to compare each of the tasks with something that stands above and beyond them all: a goal or standard. There is a simple way you can plot this out visually, as I'll illustrate by working through an example from my coaching practice:

The problem One of my clients was a stay-at-home mom who made so many to-do lists that she often ended up sitting on the sofa watching daytime television instead of doing anything. She was driven by what she thought a good mother and housewife should do but quite unable to select among all the tasks that this involved. She had no way of evaluating which of the tasks on her list were more, or less, important than each other, so no real way of deciding how best to spend her time. It was also possible that a significant item was missing from all her lists: the need for "me time." This young woman was small-chunk, in-time and outer-directed. Since every item on her to-do list seemed to relate to her overarching values, her values couldn't help her make the daily choices she had to make. Since she was in-time, she found planning very difficult and easily got overwhelmed by the sheer number of tasks on her list.

Her solution Coaching helped her work out what kinds of standards she wanted to set for her home and family (as opposed to what she had been told by her mother). That gave her benchmarks against which she could measure just how vital any one chore was. Just as important, she took on board the crucial importance of something she had previously neglected: that her family would benefit far more from a mother who had time for herself than from one who sat on the sofa in utter misery or even (if she had been able to achieve this) one who put creating an ever-immaculate house first.

EXERCISE 1 *Constellation-mapping*

A technique I used with my client was to ask her (1) to write down her underlying goal (to be a good wife and mother) in the center of a sheet of paper. Next (2) she plotted in the key meta-program habits, like moons encircling her planet-like goal. Then (3) she wrote all the things she was trying to prioritize on separate sticky notes and stuck them around the central planet. The first thing that struck her was that all the items she put down were tasks—there was nothing in there about people. But she was not actually a task-person in meta-program terms, so she was horrified, and immediately wanted to add some people-focused items: making my husband and kids comfortable; creating a restful and fun home for them to be in; having a relaxed time together. With prompting and encouragement, she also added: enjoying being with my family and, most daringly, having time for me.

Once she had included these items, her constellation was becoming pretty crowded. Was this going to be just another version of her overfull lists? The next step of the exercise (4) made a big difference: I asked her to move the sticky notes closer in or further out according to which items she felt should belong closer to the central star and which she thought were more peripheral. The people-centered

➤

ones all moved close—but so did "providing nice healthy food" and "keeping things clean."

Having her priorities physically mapped out like this kept my client mindful of what was guiding her, what meta-program defaults were driving her, and made it easier for her to sort out what was really important in managing her days.

You can use the constellation-mapping technique equally well to map out your to-do list at work, whether it's for yourself as an individual, for your team or, indeed, for the organization as a whole. You may need to use flip charts or wall boards, but the principle and the process are just the same.

One additional step you can add (5) is to run your more distant items through a "What's the worst that can happen if this doesn't get done?" check. Sometimes this allows you to remove some sticky note items from your constellation altogether!

Responding to urgency rather than importance

Urgency is a feeling, but not in itself necessarily a sufficient reason for action! Many organizations are so driven by a collective sense of urgency that, as one of my coaching clients described it, they are just running to catch up. Urgency can come from within you, or it can be passed on from others; wherever it starts it is highly contagious. What urgency does is to activate an in-time perspective, so it's a particularly powerful driver for naturally in-time people. Through-time people are likely to be impatient with others on this. Both kinds of operators need to bear in mind that both perspectives have their value.

Any feeling of urgency can be potentially valuable if you respect it as a flashing-light-on-the-dashboard signal to pause and prioritize. Think about the last time you came back to work after a holiday and found your inbox piled high. Did you plunge straight in to deal with the first, then the next? Or did you attempt to sort the items and try to deal first with what you thought might be most important? One of my clients analyzed her e-mails, and discovered that roughly a third were discards, roughly another third needed a reply but weren't high priority, and only the remaining third required both careful attention and speed. How does your inbox compare with hers? Perhaps it's worth doing your own breakdown.

EXERCISE 2 *Pull of gravity*

Use the constellation-mapping pattern a little differently to help you with this.

1. Write all your items on sticky notes as before.

2. Create two planetary centers rather than one. Label one "urgent" and the other "important." (The important center will relate to matters that are important in the long term, but not urgent now.)

3. Now allocate your items to the appropriate planetary center.

4. Take the urgent mini-constellation first. Taking each sticky-note item in turn, imagine yourself getting to the end of today without having acted on it. How much will that matter? If your answer is "not that much," imagine yourself at the end of this week without having taken action. If the answer remains "not that much," move the item to the "important" constellation. By the time you have been through all the items, you should be left with just the ones that are truly urgent.

➤

5. Now have a look at the "important" constellation. We have been assuming that "important" means "long term"—but should you start doing something about any of these right now—even if it's only making a phone call, sending an e-mail or raising the issue with someone else? If so, move them into the "urgent" constellation.

6. Now look at your urgent items again. How much time will you have to give to each? Can you do something about all of them today, tomorrow or this week? (If not, ask for help with some of them, even if help means asking someone else's permission to take something off your list.)

7. Get started!

Not saying "no" or "I've already got too much on my plate"

Just because something lands on your plate, you shouldn't assume it belongs there and accept the extra burden regardless. Your boss—or your partner or children—may all pass things on to you. Such things may have become your responsibility through custom, or maybe the other person just wants to lighten their own load. If you are externally directed, you may easily agree without even stopping to think. If you are task-focused and something clearly needs doing, you'll probably say yes. If you are a people-person and the request is going to help someone out, reassure them or fit in with what they think is important, you may happily agree, although in either case you may regret it later. Remember that whatever kind of request you're receiving and whatever kind of metaprogram habits you may have, only you can determine whether it's possible, or appropriate, for you to pick up what someone else is offering to give you.

EXERCISE 3 *Voicing your needs and wishes*

---

1. When you find yourself muttering but not actually raising the issue with the other person, check out what assumptions you are making and how they may be constraining you just as much as that extra burden does. People don't query or protest because of all kinds of reasons: they assume the other person has a right to ask because it's always been that way; because someone has to do it; because they must be overloaded themselves or they wouldn't be asking; or because they'd think me inefficient or lacking ability if I said no. Depending on the kind of issues that your internal dialogue is chewing over, if you're having this kind of discussion with yourself, your constellations could be mapped around those important twin planets, true and false, or the other significant pair, needs of self and needs of others.

2. Ask yourself what you would really like to happen. Unless you know this, you have no real basis for saying something, or for saying nothing! Do you want the other person to do the job for you? Or are you prepared to do it with help and appreciation? What is it that you're leaving unsaid?

3. Imagine you are the other person. What would be the best way to get you to understand?

4. Find a way to tell them how it is that respects both of you.

Not asking for help or for guidance in prioritizing

Even if you are sure that everything on your pile really needs doing, and doing by you, you may still be overloaded. The fatal error here is to keep your struggles to yourself. Outer-directed people can be especially prone to this, especially if they lack confidence. Bosses, colleagues, partners, children and friends can all legitimately be asked to help you. They may even be willing, or glad, to help, especially if you make it clear that you are willing to do the same for them. You might even be able to suggest a direct trade of one favor for another. "I'll do your ironing if you feed and clean out the guinea pig tonight," "I'll suggest some headings for that report if you're willing to write a couple of sentences about each of them." In planning how you could raise the issue (your approach strategy) think of someone—either in fact or fiction—whose clear but non-aggressive self-confidence you can model. How would they do it?

Finding it hard to decide between options that seem equally valid

The constellation strategy, with its different variations, should have helped you sort out your priorities in many situations, but what if a clear "winner" doesn't emerge despite all your sorting? For example, let's assume a business acquaintance asks you to attend a social event that doesn't really attract you. You feel you can't say no because the offer is kindly meant and might help cement your business relationship.

This is where in-time and through-time management can come in handy. In-time, short term, it's easier to say yes; easier because no feathers get ruffled or feelings hurt. Through-time, long term, you could be stacking up difficulties not only for yourself but for the other person and for the working relationship you have with each other. The underlying values here are honesty and trust. If you say yes while wanting to say no, your behavior will ultimately give you away. That's a rebuff for their offer, and it means they won't fully trust your word in the future. A cautiousness will have crept in between you. If you say "that's a really kind offer, but actually that's not the kind of thing I enjoy," you have recognized and rewarded their good intentions, rejecting only the specific proposal they made. You could even then follow up with a suggestion of your own for a way of getting together socially.

BECOMING PRIORITY ALERT

By definition, prioritizing is only a problem when important values or beliefs are involved, or when time is at a premium. Get into the habit of recognizing what values are involved, and what conflicts there may be either within you or between you and other people who play a part in your life. Use the constellation strategy to map out what's involved in a non-linear pattern. By mimicking the non-linear way the brain sorts itself and plots information, this can help you manage the conflicts between one value and another, one task and another, one person and another, one focus and another, one time frame and another. Effective prioritizing, when you boil it down, is essentially a question of managing relationships.

CHAPTER **15**

Negotiating

One day when I was coaching traders in an international merchant bank, I went onto the trading floor to find them all abuzz. Some of them had just returned from a negotiating course, and this one had really impressed them because the man running it was a hostage negotiator. As people whose daily negotiating could involve millions of pounds or dollars, they really respected someone like this. They recognized that he truly knew what danger and risk meant, and in their macho world this man outranked them all. Moreover, he understood that negotiating wasn't just about doing short-term deals: he had to leave both parties satisfied in the long term or, of course, further problems would arise.

In most people's experience of life at home and at work, negotiating doesn't seem to have as much at stake as lives and millions of pounds—but actually this is to grossly undervalue the impact it can have when it goes wrong and the potential it has when it goes right. Peace, harmony, cooperation and progress can result when our negotiations are successful: anger, irritation, splintering within groups, a waste of effort and resources, and failure to achieve can be some of the consequences if we get it wrong.

Negotiating is as important in building alliances and teamwork as it is in resolving differences that already exist. And developing your flexibility along three meta-programs can help you become a much more effective negotiator.

1. NEGOTIATING FROM AN AWAY-FROM SITUATION TO ONE THAT IS TOWARD

In seeking to reach agreement, people always want something, but it might be something they want to avoid, escape from or achieve in order for something else not to happen. Goals aren't always positive. People are driven by away-from motivation as well as toward, as we saw in Chapter 8. Organizations, too, have away-from goals: risk-management and quality control have an away-from fueling even in providing essential conditions in which toward goals can be pursued.

When negotiating, whether at home or at work, think about your own motivation and try to understand what may be driving the other person's. This can really help you build rapport with them before you seek to lead them. If you are not sure where they stand, try asking. A question such as "Can you explain a bit more about what you're trying to achieve here?" will give you some useful indications of whether the person is being driven by what they want to avoid (a negatively framed benefit), or whether they are being attracted toward a positively framed outcome. To achieve real progress you need to know what actual conclusion is wanted. "Stopping something" or "avoiding something" doesn't tell you this!

2. USING LARGE-CHUNK VALUES TO SOLVE SMALL-CHUNK DIFFERENCES

Small-chunk differences about specifics are quite likely to be the immediate prompt for negotiating with someone else. In organizational terms, conflicts between teams or about working arrangements can be very divisive if people focus only on the specifics (small-chunk) on which they disagree. If the discussion stays on specifics, it's unlikely that much progress can be made. Successful negotiating usually involves getting the differing parties to stop rehearsing their differences and helping them instead to recognize what they have in common. There are probably some (large-chunk) values that most people share: for example, increasing the organization's effectiveness or profitability, or being able to make their own contribution to achieving its goals.

So someone needs to help the parties find an agreement of a higher order than the differences that are troubling them to start with. In negotiations it involves moving the focus from items of detail that divide the conflicting parties toward larger issues of value or aim which are not in contention (a process known in NLP as "chunking up"). The "negotiator" doesn't have to be an outsider. Armed with your increased meta-program flexibility, you can do it yourself, even if you are one of the parties involved. The kind of issues you are looking for are ones that include, but go beyond, the very differences that are causing the problem.

HOW THEY DID IT

P. B., in a busy managerial job in social services

A client of mine, P. B., was under pressure because he was trying to hold down a busy managerial job and at the same time study for a work-related, part-time, distance-learning course. He found he was working longer hours in order to free up his weekend time for study (in the past he had often taken work home at weekends); but this wasn't really

➤

solving the problem. His boss was telling him that he should delegate more and go home earlier, but at the same time kept giving him new projects and setting urgent deadlines for their completion. My client felt that work, study and home life were all getting tangled up, and wanted to work nine longer days each fortnight in the office, devoting every tenth weekday to preparing for his course. He recognized that his boss might object on the grounds that on those tenth days he would not be available for meetings or able to deal with problems and queries at work, so in making his proposal he decided to emphasize what he and his boss had in common—some shared goals and values. They both wanted the department to function well, and my client argued that he would be more efficient at work if he separated office work and coursework more clearly. He argued that it was in the department's interests that he get the extra qualification the course was leading to. Freeing time to devote exclusively to coursework would help him study more effectively and complete the course with better grades. His boss accepted the validity of these arguments because they did indeed share the same goals and values, and agreed to the new arrangement subject to a review after three months.

EXERCISE 1 *Chunking-up strategy*

1. Start by listing topics of disagreement (usually specifics of behavior or context). Remind yourself that everyone's view is valid from where they stand.

➤

2. Then look for an area of agreement (usually principles, values or goals on which both parties agree). If you are one of the conflicting parties, this means stepping back from your feelings and taking a good, hard, objective look at what you want and what principles or values underlie it.

3. Brainstorm the alternatives. Begin to explore how the small-chunk specifics each party currently regards as important might be modified or bypassed or substituted by others that would still fulfill the same meta-level (large-chunk) function. If you and your children are bickering about homework, for example, what are the issues you might have in common? When you chunk right up, you might both agree that it's best for them to take the responsibility for their own work and for you to get out of their hair. If so, what changes would they have to make to their homework habits, and what changes would you have to make to the way you exercise your sense of parental responsibility? Both of you will have to change, but agreeing on the changes will take you forward as individuals and as a family.

If you can draw on an inventive person to help, or if you can get both parties into brainstorming mode, this will really be beneficial.

Why compromising isn't always a good thing

It is sometimes thought that negotiation has to involve compromise, but when you dig a little deeper into what people understand by "compromise" you usually find that they believe it means someone has to give up something they believe in or cherish for the sake of an alliance or a form of peace. Why would anyone choose to do that? And, if they did, how long do you think such a fudged truce would last, especially under pressure? Working from a basis of shared values helps to ensure nobody compromises over anything that fundamentally matters to them.

> 66The participants should come to see themselves as working side by side, attacking the problem, not each other.99
> ROGER FISHER AND WILLIAM URY, *Getting to Yes*, p. 11

3. IN-TIME AND THROUGH-TIME IMPLICATIONS

There are two ways to look at a trade: does it work in the short term and does it work in the long term? Short-term trades may be just that: they get you off the hook and seem to improve the situation. But do they work in the long term? I learned from the sales traders in the bank that they always needed to be mindful of this, because although they needed to make a profit on every trade if they could, they wanted the client to keep on doing business through the bank in the future. When it came to it, this could sometimes mean doing trades that were not immediately profitable for the bank. They were offsetting a short-term lack of profit against the prospect of maintaining a profitable relationship with the client long term.

When you pay your teenager for doing the ironing, mowing the lawn or cleaning the car, the short-term (in-time) benefits of the trade to both parties are obvious. But are they so obvious if you take a through-time perspective? Is your teenager learning that they only need to put something into the family "firm" if their labor is paid for—and is that something you want them to learn, remember and continue to act on?

To help you check out short-term versus long-term implications, imagine you are using the zoom lens on a camera, rapidly shifting between here and now, and there and then. You want to get both in sharp focus, as you would with a zoom, in order to check out their relative advantages and disadvantages. If you have time and space, you can make the same kind of comparison by picking a "now" place and a "future" place on a path or in a room and then stepping back and forth between them to check out immediate and future payoffs and consequences.

WHY "RIGHT AND WRONG" IS WRONG

Whatever the meta-program differences you and your negotiating partner may be operating from, there are a couple of questions you can also ask yourself, which have to do with the way you and your partner may be going about things, and which could have important repercussions on the progress and outcome of your negotiations:

1. Are you arguing about who's right or wrong?

Arguing about who's in the right can frame the situation in such a way that there has to be a loser.

> **Framing** Putting something in context in such a way as to predetermine how it is perceived. Framing can be verbal; for example, "We have some difficult decisions to make today." This implies (1) that decisions need to be made; and (2) that this will be hard to do—implicitly ruling out the possibility that not making a decision might be a valid option, or that decisions could be reached easily and harmoniously.
>
> ➤

> Framing can also be non-verbal: the elongated shape of the table in the British Cabinet room inevitably puts some Cabinet members closer to the prime minister (who sits at the middle of one long side) while others are further away, and encourages interaction between him and those close to or opposite him because they can easily catch his eye or gain his ear. Such arrangements (setting up) can be deliberate and strategic or quite unconscious.

The concepts of right and wrong are ones we learn in early childhood, at a time when both brain development and social understanding are not yet fully fledged and thinking is at a naturally black-and-white stage. It's only as we grow out of childhood that we begin to appreciate and to work with the shades of gray that more accurately reflect the complexities of adult life. Any reference to right and wrong (especially one using those very words) in adult life can easily press a button that takes a grown-up back to childlike feelings of humiliation, anger, defiance and stubbornness or even, of course, self-righteousness. None of these is a good basis for considered adult negotiation.

2. Are you making unhelpful assumptions about the other person?

The NLP developers found that people who were skilled in managing relationships tended to make neutral or favorable assumptions about other people, and to base their approach to them accordingly. NLP calls these assumptions presuppositions, because they presuppose certain conditions, thus setting the ground for the way we interact.

If we go into a negotiation (at work or at home) with negative presuppositions, we are likely to find them fulfilled.

Using a phrase like "This is going to be difficult" is quite likely to make it so. "I wonder how this will turn out" is more neutral, but it also prompts the other person to behave passively rather than actively. "I know what I'd like us to get out of this discussion, but I'm not sure how we'll get there" has a clearer progress frame while at the same time leaving the question of how the situation is to be managed more open.

> **Presuppositions** Assumptions (often unconscious) that we take into a situation and that load our verbal and non-verbal behavior so that we elicit from others what we started out expecting. In coaching clients who were angry with a colleague, friend or family member, or who made negative assumptions about that person's ability or intentions, I have often reminded them that nobody starts the day intending to be an idiot!

What meta-programs are actually involved?

Negotiation often involves more than one meta-program. Let's take a domestic example. Parents and children often come into conflict about the untidiness of the child's room. For the parent, having the house tidy is a positive (toward) goal. Most children are not interested in keeping their rooms tidy, so for the child, tidying up is at best an away-from action (anything to keep him/her off my back). Parents may assume the child is lazy, or naturally untidy, or willful, or uncooperative. Or, they are just likely to want the unwashed clothes, the old Coke bottles, and the dirty plates to be removed (away-from; small-chunk goals). Nagging doesn't work, nor moral blackmail, nor even bribery, because children assume that parents don't understand that they are more interested in (small-chunk) things like listening to music and texting friends. Curiously, there actually is a shared (large-chunk or meta-level) value at work here: each party wants freedom and independence to get on with what matters to them, without interference from the other. By making a concession in small-chunk terms based on the larger-chunk value they actually have in common, both end up getting more emotional space because they've given more emotional space.

WORKING FROM A BASE OF EQUALITY

Finally, one of the most important principles underlying all good negotiation is that of equality. Whatever your feelings, you need to assume that the other person or party has an equal right to be who they are and to want what they want. Cultivating this assumption really bears fruit: if you treat people as your equal they are much more likely to treat you as theirs, because our behavior is truly shaped by what we assume. Assuming you are equal means, too, that you will negotiate in the shared belief that you both have to be equally satisfied with the results. However frustrating negotiating can be when real differences and strong feelings are involved, reminding yourselves and each other that this is the only valid basis for an agreement that will satisfy you both—and which will last—is the best way to work with your differences rather than simply trying to settle them.

CHAPTER **16**

Beating Stress

We feel stressed when we are under pressure, either from outside forces, people or deadlines, or from internal imperatives in conflict with each other. Stress is something we feel and seek to avoid at every level. Yet you can't ensure that your life is stress-free. Stress is often a needed and valuable warning signal, telling you that you are alive and that something in you or around you is currently amiss. Dealing with it requires patient detective work in order to pinpoint what's at the bottom of it. Reducing stress is also about clarifying what you value and clearing the path toward it.

LOOKING AT STRESS FROM A NEW PERSPECTIVE

Reducing stress usually means finding new or more effective ways to manage the relationship between your situation and the way you respond to it, so that you act appropriately without your feelings disabling you or making you ineffective.

It's also to do with accepting that other people have their own agendas and may also have different ways of perceiving and managing things than you do. This is where the ability to step imaginatively into other people's shoes can help you understand both them and the situation better. Internally generated stress—the kind that results from "part of me wants this and another part of me says that" conflicts—needs similar managing: through sympathetic self-awareness and internal negotiation.

Stress is physical

Stress is a response that involves both mind and body. You can feel stressed about anything if it makes you feel pressured, harried, out-of-control or anxious. Your reactions will involve all the ingredients of the primitive flight–fight or freeze responses of early humankind, but today our stressful lifestyles cause us to experience headaches, stomachaches, palpitations and feelings of faintness, irritation or fury in response to non-physical stimuli, too.

YOUR STRESS AND YOUR META-PROGRAMS

A life without some everyday anxieties, dramas and occasional emergencies probably isn't possible. However, you can control the degree and intensity of your response to what happens within and around you. You don't have to be a victim of your circumstances or of yourself—provided you choose to self-monitor and self-regulate. As you read on, pay attention to your own responses. They will tell you where your stress is coming from and which meta-programs are involved.

Taking a step back

How much do you let things affect you (*associating* into them) as opposed to standing back and reflecting (*dissociating* from them)? If you are honest with yourself, haven't there been moments when you have felt at the tipping point—the point where you were on the verge of losing your temper or getting upset—and when you felt justified in *letting yourself go* over that edge? I have stressed those words "letting yourself go" because for most of us, most of the time, there really is a choice, and if we're honest we are aware of it right there and then. There are always reasons that feel sufficient; and often we actually allow ourselves to feel stressed in order to make a point, whether that point is made for our own sake or as a message to someone else. In everyday tensions as well as actual emergencies, the ability to dissociate from your own feelings, however momentarily, can help you assess the situation dispassionately and then respond appropriately.

Knowing how to monitor and manage the extent to which you are associated into your feelings or strategically dissociated from them can help you spare yourself the unpleasantness of feeling stressed, while retaining the option of making your point in a more direct, and usually more effective, way. You do have a choice—even if it comes after your feelings have overwhelmed you. Just recognizing that they have can be your signal to begin your distancing process.

Understanding others

The same is true for other people. When someone's feelings (however appropriate) are making things difficult for them or for those around them, first make sure they know that you respect what they are going through—and then try to help them shift to a more dispassionate place where they can assess the situation and begin to manage it more effectively. NLP calls this process "shifting perceptual positions."

Shifting perceptual positions Examining a situation from different perspectives: your own (first position), someone else's (second position), and from that of an objective observer (third position).

Shifting perceptual positions can be really helpful when you or those around you are frustrated. In anyone's work or home life, there will be times when routines are interrupted, rules get broken, or other people "fail" to do what they are "supposed" or "ought" to do. Procedural people are going to feel disturbed, irritated or upset by this; inventive people are more likely to frame the unexpected or unwanted as challenges they can address and even meet. However, they too can be frustrated (stressed) by what they may think of as "petty restrictions" or "letter of the law" requirements. It helps to remember that people have their own reasons for responding the way they do.

Time management and stress reduction

In-time people will often find time keeping and time management stressful because these demand through-time skills, which they don't have or don't have enough of. On the other hand, they can be much less pressured about sequencing and planning than someone who works to a through-time schedule! Whichever type of time traveler you are, the knack is to arrange your life so that you minimize getting into the situations you find hard to handle. At work, people can feel pressured (stressed) by the need to meet short-time deadlines, but if you are able to place short-term tasks and needs within a longer-term, more strategic, context, this may help you feel more relaxed as well as better able to prioritize.

Which direction are you coming from?

Stress is a form of friction, when someone has to choose between meeting their own needs or wishes and fitting in with those of other people. This can affect both inner-directed people and outer-directed ones. Groundbreakers, men or women who want to step out of fixed gender roles and responsibilities, managers who want to remain "one of the boys" in relation to the people they manage, and those who seem to be square pegs in round holes will be just as affected as outer-directed people who are "programmed" to fit in but who may have a sneaking feeling that their own wishes are being neglected or jettisoned.

Fear (away-from) is stressful. Ambition (toward) can be, too. So can wanting without much prospect of having, or feeling excited about the prospect of something new without the time, energy or money to pursue it. Whether you trip up because you are looking backward over your shoulder or because you are looking fixedly ahead, you may not see what's right in front of you. Either way, the experience of tripping is much the same! Understanding your default and appreciating other people's allows you to game your response more appropriately to the needs of the immediate situation while at the same time giving you the chance to develop a strategic view of where your actions here and now might lead in the future.

Once you appreciate what the situation involves, you have a choice. Knowing which meta-programs are influencing you (and others) means that you can manage the situation rather than being managed by it.

COMMON STRESS ISSUES

Each of the following issues may involve more than one meta-program.

Poor time management

To feel hurried is to feel harried, whether the cause is your own inability to manage time or the fact that someone else has overloaded you or derailed your schedule. If there aren't enough hours in the day, check what you and others expect, consider how you manage time yourself, and reprioritize. Your opportunity for effective action is now. If you can hang onto this instead of fretting about the past or worrying about the future, you will be more able to make the most of present opportunities—and in the process almost certainly find yourself becoming less stressed.

Caring too much or too little

Feelings are always appropriate—to *something*. Stress is always in proportion—to *something*. If you—or other people—seem to be getting more worked up about something than you or they think it really warrants, move away from the specifics and ask what issues, or what history, is involved. We often get upset or angry when our feelings of self, or our deeply held values, are involved, even though the issue may seem more trivial in itself. Equally, something that happened today can easily make any of us feel the same way we did years ago. Acknowledging that stress legitimately relates to something, even if that something isn't immediately obvious, allows you to begin inquiring, of yourself or of others, what that something might be, and opens up the possibility of dealing with the real, not just the apparent, causes.

If, on the other hand, caring too little seems to be the issue, it's probably because you have different priorities from someone else or because you haven't put enough effort into imagining how the other person might be feeling. Or it may be that you haven't made sure they know you respect their feelings, even though you may have to act against them. By taking second position and letting them know you are trying to see where they are coming from, you remove a cause of stress that is not inherent in the situation itself. This leaves both of you free to deal with whatever stress genuinely belongs there.

This scenario also applies the other way round: if you feel stressed because someone at home or work isn't taking your feelings or your experience into account, you don't have to suffer (and resent) in silence. We don't have the right to assume that other people are mind-readers, however nice and helpful that might be. Just tell them.

If even you think you are caring too little in the situation, it may be that you are dissociating in order to prevent yourself experiencing unpleasant feelings (such as anger or resentment) that you anticipate it bringing up. Don't give yourself a hard time for being "hard" or "heartless": making yourself feel bad about how you are fixes nothing! Just do what you need to now and take time for reflection, if needed, later on.

Feeling inadequate

We often feel stressed when we are expected to do something but feel doubtful of our ability to deliver. This kind of stress is a compound of performance anxiety ("How will I look?" "What if I can't . . . ?") and a fear of how we will be judged ("What will they think?") if we tell someone we are inexperienced, unskilled, overloaded or just plain scared. In other words, it usually involves some aspect of inner vs. outer directedness. Giving the other person a chance to hear how you feel and hopefully understand it is usually better in the long run. One of the things I've learned in the years I've worked as a therapist and coach is that the world is full of able, competent, responsible, authoritative and even important people who all feel inadequate far more often than they may have you believe. How would it be if we acknowledged to ourselves and others that feeling inadequate is part of being human—and then got on with doing what we want or have to do?

Not being able to say no

Many, perhaps most, people are anxious about saying no because they fear disapproval or even rejection. Those moments when your heart is saying no while your mouth is about to say yes are a brief but important opportunity to reduce the stress that conflict is causing you, but you can only do it if you observe and acknowledge the message your heart is giving you. (A similar conflict can also happen when your heart is saying yes and your head is saying no.) Even if you can't immediately get the "difficult" word out, you can usually buy time—from other people or even yourself—to think more carefully before giving an answer. Even a little through-time bargaining for delay can help you out. (There is more about this in Chapter 20.)

Overall, although stress is an uncomfortable thing, it is often your warning that something needs to be attended to, changed or fixed. Using your meta-program understanding and flexibility to appreciate where the stress is coming from and what it is signaling is both the quickest and the most effective way to reduce or remove it.

HOW THEY DID IT

Jo and Jim

A coaching client of mine found his partner's "lackadaisical" approach to time infuriating. His partner was never ready when it was time to leave for an appointment or social event, and so they were almost invariably late. My client was very through-time, and he felt this discrepancy strongly, though his in-time partner was quite laid-back about it. Nagging didn't work, neither did having considered

➤

conversations at times when punctuality was not actually an immediate issue. In the end, my client decided that he couldn't change his partner, but he could change himself. He worked out a number of practical strategies that made this possible. First, he reminded himself how much he valued and appreciated his partner in many other ways, and acknowledged that these were actually deeper and more significant to him. Second, he suggested to his partner that they should, where possible, avoid trying to meet specific deadlines. By openly talking with friends about their differing approaches to time, they were often able to negotiate more flexible arrival times and so avoid disappointing themselves and others. Where a real deadline existed, my client decided that he would nudge his partner along by giving an earlier "leaving-by" time or by over-estimating how long it would take them to get there. In combination, these strategies took away many of the practical difficulties their contrasting timings had caused, and greatly reduced stress for them both.

CHAPTER **17**

Hiring and Firing

Although "hiring and firing" sounds like a work issue, we can also be faced with similar issues and tactical choices when taking people into our private lives or easing them out again. Think about partners, relatives and friends. The choices you make in getting involved with them, making them a part of your life, or deciding that you don't want to be involved with them any longer are not really dissimilar to the choices you make at work: employing, being employed, managing and being part of work groups, sorting out interpersonal difficulties, or eventually perhaps having to terminate your or their employment. I have had plenty of work clients considering issues like these—and I have also had clients who realized they had similar issues to address in their private lives, the most dramatic of these being whether or not to break away from their partners, children or parents—usually after many failed attempts to tackle the difficulties between them. Many people experience the additional complication of having to separate from, or divorce, someone while still having to continue relating to that same person over the long term to manage childcare, visits, financial support and decisions about education.

FINDING AN OBJECTIVE VIEWPOINT

If at first it seems strange, even cold, to think of close relationships in this way, ask yourself what you might gain from attempting to slot some of your "close" relationships into the kind of template that is appropriate at work. What might be some of the important issues that both have in common? The value of taking this analytical approach is that it can help you dissociate from some of the complex and powerful feelings that you and others may be experiencing. At work someone's performance is usually going to be measured against some agreed criteria, and in many firms there will be an annual or six-monthly review with their manager to assess how they are doing. Such a review often also includes a discussion of what should be in their PDP (personal development plan) for the upcoming year and what support, training or target-setting will help them improve within their role. If they fail to meet the criteria specified by their contract, they could be given an informal or, later, even a formal warning, after which continued non-performance could result in being let go.

Imaginatively engaging with the audacious idea that such a process might also benefit some of our nearest and dearest—and even ourselves in our relationships with them—can actually help us to become clearer during the stages of the problem-solving process where we observe, reflect and experiment. The key element is establishing and then sticking to what you both share. As Peter Senge says:

> Few, if any, forces in human affairs are as powerful as shared vision. At its simplest level, a shared vision is the answer to the question, "What do we want to create?" . . .
> A shared vision is a vision that many people are truly committed to, because it reflects their own personal vision.
>
> *The Fifth Discipline*, p. 206

And this is true of good relationships at work and at home.

Contracts

The basis of any relationship is a contract between the parties, whether or not it is explicitly articulated in words or spelled out in detail. Such implied agreements underlie our personal relationships, even though the idea may initially seem inappropriate or even shocking. What actually is the nature of the contract? What does each party expect of the other? My husband and I once had a late-night conversation about what we felt we could ask of our different friends, and what we would feel able to do, or not do, for them. Who would volunteer an airport pickup? Whose cars might be confidently loaned or borrowed? Who would trust whom enough to lend, or give, them money? (We have friends who generously gave us a no-return check when we were in dire straits. Later, we did the same for another friend in financial trouble.) Who could talk to whom about what? In other words, what was the implicit contract underlying our different friendships? At work, similar discussions can be had within teams or between managers and their staff as to what each expects of the other.

How well is the contract understood? How much is explicit and how much is read between the lines? Do both parties understand what's expected of them? Do they agree to those expectations, and are they capable of meeting them? Problems in this area are often indicated by comments like "But I thought that . . ." or "They seemed to expect me to . . ." In NLP such implicit bundles of meaning are called complex equivalents.

Complex equivalents are like the containers on each side of weighing scales: on the one hand, there is always an abstract idea (like "loyalty," "initiative" and "support") and on the other there are the specifics of what someone believes this actually equates to in practice. For example, "loyalty"

►

can equate to "not telling anyone else about what goes on behind our front door," "standing up for anyone in our family/our team even when we know they are in the wrong," "not selling trade secrets" or "not taking a day off in forty years." Since different people can use the same word to equal different things (sometimes very different things), it's possible for them to misunderstand each other quite profoundly over specifics while agreeing with each other that "loyalty" or "hard work" are important. Any problems tend to arise from differences in the specifics!

- What happens if (when) either party fails to live up to their side of the contract? If the implied "contract" of a marriage originally was that the wife should give up work to look after the children, what happens when she decides to take a part-time degree? If the implicit contract of a team leader's appointment was that she'd be there to lead and develop her team for some time, what happens when she almost immediately becomes pregnant?

- How well do the parties to the contract dovetail with each other in terms of skills and values? Is it a good thing or a limiting one if your work team all have similar values and attitudes (and perhaps similar meta-program defaults, too)? Has anyone considered what those shared values and attitudes are good for and whether they may be limiting? Did anybody think about this as each appointment was made, and is it part of the thinking in connection with any future appointments?

- Do "employees" respect and value each other where they differ (or even specifically for those differences)?

- How is the contract going to be maintained or, if necessary, enforced?

All of these issues can, and probably should, be discussed openly at some time—preferably a time when everyone is calm and reflective rather than frustrated or cross because someone else has breached the implied agreement between them. Even then, explaining what you expected and asking what they thought can surface some of the buried assumptions and help you both reach a clearer understanding and a better-founded agreement for the future.

Families often have quite complex systems of implied contracts, and a key value they often embody is "fairness." When one partner gets irritated about something apparently "trivial," like whose turn it is to load the dishwasher, it's usually because they feel the other has gotten away with doing less than they should have: it just isn't fair. The word "should" usually implies that some kind of contract is involved! As children grow up they become involved in contracts, too: taking a share of household chores can be expected in implied exchange for what they're given or what's done for them in other ways.

You can usefully stand back (take third position) to help you get clear and stay clear any time you need to take stock of what's at stake in a relationship. Dissociating from your immediate feelings like this can also be helpful if you are outer-directed and feel at risk of being overruled or overwhelmed by your own "oughts and shoulds" or by the forcefulness of others. If, on the other hand, you always know exactly what you want and are usually rather too inclined to trample your way to get it, then second-positioning the other person(s) involved to check how you might come across to them will allow you to get enough of a feel for (associate into) their world to prevent friction, disappointment or pain on either side.

HAVING THE COURAGE TO MOVE ON

Human beings are creatures of habit, in relationships as much as in anything else; and for a variety of reasons we can hang on to relationships that aren't doing us any favors. Old friends or colleagues who bore us or drain our energy, whom we continue to see for old time's sake or because we feel sorry for them, or because we have always met up at Christmas since the year dot . . . these are all reasons why unsatisfactory relationships continue. You will know at once if there's anyone like this in your life. In a work setting, perhaps you employ or work alongside someone who, although loyal, is no longer quite up to the job, who doesn't realize the world is changing and who takes up their colleagues' time by their slowness, need for reassurance, a tendency to gossip, and so on. Continuing to have someone like this around you without addressing the underlying "hire and fire" issues they raise can drain and debilitate you, depressing your spirits and eating up your energy and zest. They can make you depressed.

Firing someone from your work life or home life is rarely simple and you can feel unfair or even unjustified. The meta-program tension isn't just one between inner- (self) and outer- (other or external value-based) directedness. There's also an important away-from–toward opportunity involved. Some-one who drains you depletes the potential energy and drive you have available for moving toward positive things like achievement, excitement, satisfaction, ambition, purpose and contentment in any sphere. If you are naturally a toward person, they can really put a damper on you. If you are naturally away-from, you may be able to harness that aver-sive energy to withdraw from them, cut them off, or shunt them sideways. If you feel guilty about losing contact with someone, or even ceasing contact entirely, remind yourself that nobody really benefits from a relationship unless both parties do.

OVERLAPPING AND CONTRASTING PERSONALITIES

When people are closely involved with each other on a regular basis, as in families, friendships and at work, any differences in key sorting mechanisms can make for trouble. The "cover-your-backside" person (away-from) will lack understanding with the "can-do" (toward) person; the inventive person may feel their ideas are thwarted by their procedural colleague or boss; the task-person can be thought heartless by the more soft-centered people-person; "similar" and "different" people will experience the same situation and take contrasting information from it, as will those who are associated or dissociated; in-time and through-time people will act and prioritize differently. On the other hand, contrasting approaches can bring freshness, vitality, new perspectives and fun into life at work and at home. It all depends on how such contrasts are managed.

In hiring people, whether at home or at work, you need to know what role they are to play and what expectations both you and they have of this, and, of course, what they are expecting your contribution to the contractual relationship to be. Selecting people whose ways of operating are just like yours can mimimize stress in both domestic and work contexts, but it can also potentially make life more bland and lacking in stretch and stimulus. If you "appoint" people whose meta-program defaults strongly contrast with your own, you can run the risk of polarizing more and more as time goes by. This happened to a couple I once worked with. Initially they were attracted by their differences—he was calm and rational and she was warm, lively and challenging—but as the years went by he came to despise her for being "over-emotional" while she began to loathe and pity his "coldness" and lack of feeling.

Dovetailing skills can be one good way to manage differences—provided the individuals' differences can be managed so that they genuinely complement each other. As important, you need to identify, honor and if possible make full use of your work and home team members' individual strengths—which includes their meta-program default settings—as well as trying to take pressure off their limitations. This is quite a demand to make of yourself, but it can also make home and work life less frustrating and more harmonious.

WHAT USUALLY GOES WRONG IN HIRING AND FIRING

A contract that is vague will create difficulties for both parties. Preparing one that is clear and listening to your own intuition can help you both negotiate difficult decisions.

A contract that lacks clarity

When you take someone on, what do you expect of them, and what do they think is expected of them? Employment contracts are written down, but even they often lack the clarity that's needed to help both parties build a satisfactory working relationship. Where personal relationships are involved, many people can be reluctant to make the contract clear by spelling out what they want and expect from each other, not just because doing this may carry legalistic overtones but because they fear that somehow it implies a lack of trust, or even affection. This is absolutely not the case. Telling someone clearly what you need, want or expect from them is actually giving them the recipe for succeeding.

Whatever kind of contract is involved, complex equivalents like "support" or "assist," "initiate" or "take responsibility for" all need spelling out so that the "job-holder" knows the criteria they have to meet, and the "employer" has an assurance that the job will be done as they want. Friendships and parent–child relationships may need their implicit contracts revisiting and revising over time as circumstances change.

Not listening to your intuition

Even where a contract is specific and the criteria are met, it's possible to choose the wrong friends or the wrong colleagues. We never have all the information, but we do have another source that we can't afford to ignore. That's our intuition, gut feeling, or unconscious summing-up of a person, and it may point you toward issues and criteria you haven't thought to specify. The person seems to fit with your needs, but other things can also be involved and can make all the difference: for example, what's their energy level? How well will they fit with your hyperactive, go-getting team, or your quiet, reflective family group? Does this extra sense of yours tell you that this person will fit in, or stick out? Non-rational judgments are just that: non-rational. This doesn't mean they should be ignored. Snap judgments are just that—they arrive in your consciousness well before any evidence that may support them. Nonetheless there always is evidence, registered behind any gut feeling. You just need to trust that, given time, it will surface and should be factored in to any decisions you have to make.

Now that you know about meta-programs and how they work, you are in a great position to make people choices that work and last.

What meta-program profiles would be fun in a friend, useful in a potential appointee, or life-enhancing in a partner? What kind of a person do you want to have around you, and among you? What would be your person spec? What combinations have you found hardest to deal with? How can you use your developing meta-program flexibility to minimize conflict and increase understanding if you have to deal with them in the future?

WHAT CHOICES DO YOU HAVE IN YOUR FAMILY?

So far I've talked about situations in which we can choose whether to have someone around us or not. However, families we opt into through partnership and create through parenting present choices that are often harder: put up, shut up, try to change or—where all else fails—reject. Knowing more about how you and others sort information helps pinpoint differences and the sources of potential conflict, which in itself gives you more choices about how to manage yourself and how you can understand others. Of course you can go on being irritated by the way your father-in-law refers to your kids as "my kids." Asking yourself if he is just expressing his devotion to them or if he is really trying to gain control of them (as your worst fantasies suggest) gets you looking for evidence, for points of true similarity or real difference, and that gets you thinking about what you can do and how you can approach him differently in the future. Of course, you can allow your grown-up child back home when he loses his job or can't get one after college. How are you and he going to manage the situation so that it works for both of you? In NLP there's a phrase that sums up what you are looking for: "influencing with integrity." In both cases, you may not feel you have a choice about cutting the person out of your life, and you may not want to. But you don't have to put up and shut up either. Your meta-program understanding is a basis for approaching the other person with a base of respect—for them and for yourself—that gives you the best chance of working things out effectively together.

USING THE PROBLEM-SOLVING SEQUENCE

When you really need to lose someone from your life, this sequence can help make your firing as effective as your hiring, even though it may feel more daunting. Your starting place is just the same: observing and understanding the situation from a third-person viewpoint that allows you to take a detached view of your own feelings and to respect differences even where they are causing problems. Reflecting on what you have observed helps you decide what you need to do. In human terms, the actual or potential relationship belongs to both parties, which is why the right reasons for firing can be just as positive a step as the right reasons for hiring. Even if firing the employee, separating from your partner or ending a friendship makes your heart beat faster, your palms sweat and your stomach sink, both of you will ultimately benefit from changing or ending something unsatisfactory—and perhaps from understanding why and how it went wrong.

An invaluable skill for anyone to cultivate is the skill of "bottom-lining," which means sharing your dispassionate assessment of the situation with the other person involved.

> **Bottom-lining** Making clear just how things stand in terms of profit and loss. Originally drawn from accounting, this metaphor helps us understand that the bare "figures" of a situation are just that: a statement of fact.

The art of bottom-lining is twofold: to keep the factual statement to a minimum and keep it free of emotional loading. It should provide a baseline (finance again) of understanding upon which any further action can be built. Its essence is factual accuracy, clarity, simplicity, an absence of being judgmental, and overall a clearly conveyed respect for the other person. As soon as you start to share your reflections, you are beginning the process of testing and evaluation. Making your hitherto private assessment explicit in itself changes the dynamic of the relationship, whether you are telling someone why you want them in your life or why you would prefer them out of it. Either way, they are going to respond, so you'll soon get more evidence about the appropriateness of your judgment and the effectiveness of how you are handling the situation, which will tell you what, if anything, you need to adjust. If you bottom-lined well when you fired someone, the chances are that you and the other person will remain on speaking terms if you meet again. If you bottom-lined well when you hired someone, you will have helped them understand just what it was about them that made you pick them to be part of your life—and understanding that can enrich their self-esteem and self-confidence. Bottom-lining isn't just for work. When it highlights something you value in someone else it can deepen the relationship, and when it pinpoints something that is causing difficulty it can be an opportunity for enlightenment and change.

Essentially, both hiring and firing are about managing the process of engagement and disengagement that's implicit in all human relationships. Understanding meta-programs gives you two advantages: you will appreciate more fully how different people filter information, and you will also be able to use specific meta-program skills to manage the challenges and pitfalls that choosing people can involve.

HOW THEY DID IT
A good divorce

A couple had been married for a number of years before they had any children. They had lived abroad and both worked full-time, and though there were some tensions in

➤

the relationship they got along pretty well. After their child was born, however, things became more difficult. The wife gave up her job, and they began to realize that talking about work (they were in the same industry but in different companies) had provided much of the daily small change of their relationship. By the time their daughter was three, it was clear that the marriage had worn thin. Being calm and adult people, they sat down to decide how they were going to manage, and devised arrangements that would allow each of them to go on playing an important part in their daughter's life. The husband found a apartment a few miles away, so that he could visit and babysit regularly as well as having the little girl for his share of weekends. When things broke in his former home, he often came round to fix them. Both parents attended school events, either separately or together, and took turns in ferrying their daughter to out-of-school activities. It wasn't always easy, but they were united in wanting to be the best parents they could, and to ensure that their daughter didn't lose out just because they no longer felt able to live with each other. Over the years both continued to maintain regular contact with their in-laws, with whom they had good relationships, attending family events such as golden wedding celebrations and funerals. Many years later the man remarried, but continued to spend part of every Christmas with his ex-wife and daughter. Later still, they began to join him and his new wife on such occasions. Despite their differences, they had worked together to turn a poor marriage into a good divorce.

I called this chapter "hiring and firing" to emphasize that relationships involve choice. At the extremes, we can opt in and we can opt out. Being aware that we do have both possibilities within our control means that we feel freer to do what we mostly want and need to do, which is to manage the middle ground. We got into this relationship—whether at work or at home. How can we now make the best of it? In giving us the concept of modeling and the tools to do it, NLP can increase our confidence in discovering, developing and using strategies that make relationships work. The models for good practice that we draw on can come from books, friends, or the careful observation of others. Understanding how meta-programs work and becoming more flexible in the way we use them ourselves opens up our choices still further. NLP reminds us that the essential basis for all effective relationships remains the same: honesty coupled with non-judgmental respect.

CHAPTER **18**

Teamwork

Building a team takes forward many of the issues and strategies I've explored in Chapter 17. Yes, you may know how to hire and fire individuals, but what about building a team? In one-to-one relationships you always have a degree of control, but once you have assembled a group of people (whether family, friends or at work) most of the interaction will be going on between them. Is it possible to influence processes you aren't involved in, and may not even know about? If so, how can your meta-program understanding help you? How can you influence a dynamic entity of which you are only a small part?

Only rarely can you set up an entire team from the beginning: friends come packaged with their partners, children or entire family and social networks, each of whom has a direct or indirect impact on the relationship that friend has with you. You inherit one family (parents, relatives and siblings) and when you "appoint" a partner you also acquire the package of people that comes with them. You may create children, but even from birth they are their own people, interacting with each other and with their friends. Even at work, it's rare to be able to set up a team from scratch. All this means that there is a lot you don't, and can't, control.

GOOD INFLUENCES

Control, in fact, is a no-no concept. Influence is more accurate—and more achievable. NLP reminds us that we cannot *not* influence others—the only question is how. There are a number of significant things you can do to set up the kind of teamwork you want and to help keep it on track. You can make your expectations, intentions and goals explicit (see pages 218–9); you can model the way you want team members to relate to each other (see page 173); and you can bottom-line it (see page 226) when they (or you) don't. You can also have it as your underpinning rule in every aspect of team-building, teamwork and team maintenance that people are encouraged to recognize and work to their own and others' strengths, which of course include their meta-program preferences. If you repeatedly model these behaviors in every interaction you have with any member of your team, you begin to create habits and expectations that can ripple through the team network in a beneficial way. Good habits get built in the same way as bad ones—by frequent repetition.

- If you point out (bottom-line) non-respect whenever you encounter it, you help challenge behavior that threatens team cohesion and support. Include toward people by pointing out how much recognition and appreciation helps everyone work to their best. You don't have to be the official team leader to do this and you don't have to work yourself up for a major discussion—often short, throwaway comments can do the trick: "I'm sure she'd love to hear how helpful you found her when . . . ," for example, can help create a ripple of praise and boost the self-esteem of the giver ("Aren't I nice?") and the receiver ("I never realized he appreciated me").

- Cover away-from people by pointing out that you're sure they wouldn't want to be thought of as obstructive or undermining, and imply how they could rectify this with a throwaway suggestion such as "Do you think he might find that disheartening given how much time he's put in?"

BUILDING A TEAM ON ITS STRENGTHS

In recent years a whole body of strengths-based research and writing has emerged, developed initially by the Gallup Organization as a result of two massive research studies over the last 25 years of the 20th century. They were investigating what employees wanted from their workplaces, and it involved thousands of hours of interviewing, followed by the collection of many thousands of questionnaire responses. As a result they published the first "strengths-based" books: *First Break All the Rules—What the World's Greatest Managers Do Differently* (2001) and *Now, Discover Your Strengths* (2002). This research clearly showed that it is rarely worthwhile trying to correct people's "weaknesses" and much more valuable for everyone concerned to identify someone's natural, built-in talents and place them where they can be most fully used. (For some inspirational and practical books on this subject, see Further Reading.)

The strengths-based literature led to the identification of a range of specific natural talents that seem to be built in, and which I'd argue actually work through the specific meta-program patterns that this book is exploring. Someone who is, for example, a "maximizer" in strengths terms is likely to have a strong toward patterning. (Maximizers are naturally attracted to what is already good and seek to make it even better.) Someone whose talent is for "winning others over" is likely to operate a subtle balance between their inner-directed clarity about what they want and an outer-directed understanding of how that very same goal could be represented as being in the other person's interest, too.

I believe that people's individual patterns of meta-programming are part of their unique strengths "profile," and as such lend bias which feeds into the life work of any teams they belong to. Just as a weed is only a flower in the wrong place, a meta-program or a strength is in itself neutral. In the wrong place it can distort or block a team's effectiveness, while in the right place it can help it flourish. Someone who is brilliant on one end of a meta-program spectrum usually needs counterbalancing within a team by someone with a contrasting "take" on things. Each approach is potentially valuable, but they aren't usually enough on their own. By noticing, benchmarking and, where appropriate, helping other people to understand how different individuals' complex clusters of meta-program patterns operate at work and at home, you can do your bit to select, manage and support them as part of your team.

Building confidence in yourself and others

Understanding your own profile is hugely valuable: learning to recognize and understand the profiles of others is a further step again. Whatever your status or role in a team, you can educate other members into this kind of awareness just by making naturalistic and informal comments that draw attention to the similar and different ways people operate.

When people are helped to identify their unique strengths profile—whether it's talents-based or meta-program-based—they immediately feel more confident

➤

and more accepted. They are no longer having to try to be something they aren't. They are not being asked to spend time and energy trying to fix what are considered their weaknesses, and they aren't asking each other to, either. This removes a great deal of anxiety, stress and frustration from everyone. It also encourages them to think carefully, and often deeply, about the contribution they can make to the life and work of the team, just by committing their energies and their unique viewpoints and skills to its endeavors. This is just as true for friends, families, partners and children as it is of colleagues at work. People can discover their strengths by reading *Now, Discover Your Strengths* and completing an online questionnaire it gives access to. Or you can introduce friends, family and colleagues to the concept of meta-program patterning through talking about it, telling them about your own or, of course, by showing them this book! You don't have to get technical—for most meta-programs you don't even have to use the NLP labels. People easily accept the idea of "procedures" vs. "inventiveness" or "broad-brush" vs. "detail" if they are introduced in relation to something that's going on at the time (explaining why someone saw a situation so differently from someone else, for example). Usually, they will find the idea fascinating, and may even ask to know more. If they don't, you will still have sown the seeds of the idea, and can return to it later.

WHAT USUALLY GOES WRONG

Building a successful team involves a number of important things: getting the right skill sets and mixes, choosing people who share the values and principles the team is there to support or promote, and helping the team gel as a social entity. Getting this right is complex—especially since team-building at work often focuses just, or primarily, on the skills or skills-and-ethics parts. A number of problems can arise as a result.

Teams selected only for their task skills

Problems arise when the team has not been assembled with regard to any "fit" or complementary features between them. Instead, individuals have been selected largely or only on the basis of their task-related skills.

A team is a living and dynamic entity. It is a social system in which every part influences, and is influenced by, others. If you fail to appreciate this, you will have no idea what kind of final result you are going to turn out—and it could just be a disaster! Teams once formed settle into their own ways of functioning (human beings are creatures of habit), so whenever anyone leaves or joins, the accustomed balance will be upset. Think of the "hole" made in a marriage when a child (or children) leaves home, of the changes in power that can happen when someone leaves a work team, of the adjustments that are necessary to friendship networks when couples split up or reform, of the feelings of loss, uncertainty, relief and perhaps also rebellion when one team leader leaves and another is appointed. These changes need to be addressed directly and openly by the remaining team members.

The team members are too similar

As one of my clients, the manager of an international media team, said to me, "My team all think alike, so we have very little friction. Everyone gets on with everyone else and they do a good job. At the moment this overlap works for us, but I'm also aware that in some circumstances it might limit us, too." She had it in a nutshell: what clearly worked in the existing circumstances might not have been so successful if the situation changed. There was no flexibility or "marginal cover" built in. In business today, there is an inherent risk in establishing teams with narrowly homogeneous skill sets (which includes their meta-program habits), because they will not be as sensitive to weak signals that herald shifts they should respond to. Slowness in responding may render what they do and how they do it less appropriate in the future. (There's more on this in Chapter 19.)

The team members don't respect each other's differences

No team can work at its best unless its members respect each other. That doesn't mean they have to see things the same way, but it does mean they have to base their teamwork on the assumption that different views are valid in themselves. This means separating validity from effectiveness: for example, the person who at work can develop a visionary goal for the future of the company (inventive, toward, through-time) may well lack the interest to put essential practical details in place (procedural, in-time, small-chunk) for it to be achieved, and could dismiss this degree of minutiae as boring. A team member good at detail (small-chunk) and procedure may be struggling to understand how the large-chunk vision of greater accountability or transparency will affect their daily behavior and goals at work, and could dismiss the vision as impractical or airy-fairy. Both need to adopt a wider framework in which differences are honored if they are to complement and benefit each other at work or at home. Time issues can be a problem within family or friendship teams, too, where some through-time members get exasperated with in-time members who tend to be late or to overrun, while the latter feel nagged to cut short what they are currently doing or enjoying.

They take each other for granted

When this happens team members fail to recognize and reward each other's contributions to the team and its work.

In many family and work cultures, praising and rewarding people verbally are not seen as an important part of everyday relating to each other. They may do so on special occasions or perhaps because someone has done something extra or outstanding, but not for just doing the job, or just being a reliable friend, a good partner or a helpful child. Coaching over a period of years in a large international bank, I more than once heard people say, "No one praises me—they just say, 'If you weren't good you wouldn't be working here—what more recognition do you want?'" There seems to be an underlying assumption here that if you keep telling others how special or valuable they are, they might become bigheaded.

Actually, this doesn't tend to happen. Rather, the reverse is true. Because people tend to interpret no feedback as negative feedback, being negative around others—which includes not acknowledging their actions and qualities—can negatively impact performance, morale and even health quite seriously. (For more on this, see *How Full Is Your Bucket* in the Bibliography.) If, on the other hand, people are lucky enough to experience a culture of acknowledgment, the positive consequences are equally demonstrable.

A lack of understanding about the way people do things

Team members (including any manager) may not understand and utilize differences in the way people handle information and approach things.

Praise is nice—focused praise is even better. Tom Rath and Donald Clifton, the authors of *How Full Is Your Bucket*, say, "What we recognize in others helps them shape their identity and their future accomplishments." Praise that specifically highlights the way someone thinks and acts (how their meta-programs are played out in the way they do things at work or at home) contributes to them as individuals and reinforces their contribution to the team in a very usable way.

What kind of identity and what kind of accomplishments do you want to encourage in your team?

Failing to address issues when they arise

People fail to raise issues with each other, and let things go until something just "blows."

A pretty strong away-from motivation is at work here—most people are afraid of the potential "confrontation" or "conflict" that may arise from giving "negative feedback." The words in quotation marks show the away-from drive behind not saying anything. Teamwork of all kinds is often bedeviled by people's unwillingness or lack of skill in attempting bottom-lining (see page 226). When they are fed up or irritated with someone else, they all too often back down and put up with the situation. Unfortunately, this means that their feelings don't get dealt with, and the offending behavior can recur because the other person hasn't been told about its effects or been given any guidance as to what else they might do. So there's a powder keg waiting to blow up when another spark comes its way. Giving someone the bottom line regarding how the situation is at the moment and telling them what would be better gives them the chance to get things right.

Too focused on the task or habit

The team is task-focused (or habit-focused) and forgets that it needs attention and maintenance.

Work teams, family teams and social teams can all get so busy with their everyday activities (in-time and small-chunk focus) that they neglect the longer-term (large-chunk and through-time) need to maintain the team itself.

Big firms often organize away-days, or even team-bonding events, in an attempt to address the team as a dynamic entity. Families go on outings and holidays to unwind and spend quality time with each other. Commonly, such events are both infrequent and special: it's as though people are assuming that bonding, quality time and unwinding can't be a regular feature of team existence. Teams need maintenance just like any material structure, and maintenance is best done frequently and routinely. Team members often prefer to cancel a team meeting because of a lack of "business," where no specific discussion items have been proposed, rather than take the opportunity to make the team itself the business of the meeting. Families with lots of outside interests can do the same, and may not prioritize daily times together because they don't see them as important. One family I knew recognized this and agreed that whatever else they were doing they would all have breakfast together every day.

Team maintenance is about openness and appreciation. It doesn't take much to halt or reverse the lowering of morale and energy that happens as a result of everyday pressure, frustration and taking people or actions for granted. Without oil, mechanisms dry out and grind to a halt. Without water, plants shrivel and die. Without recognition, people do much the same. You can set yourself to cultivate extra acts of generosity like those I've been talking about, but if it suits you more you can make a habit of saying thank you for the smallest, most routine acts of cooperation and helpfulness. It can all be small stuff, but it adds up. Small-chunk does actually become large-chunk! Where teams operate on a basis of trust and recognition, dealing with friction or problems as they occur, and spending time and effort on building, reviewing and maintaining their internal relationships, they can indeed add up to more than the sum of their parts.

HOW THEY DID IT

The Jago family

My husband, Leo, is the eldest of six children, born and raised in New Zealand where his family still lives. He told me that his mom, Alice, was a great manager. When they were young, every child had jobs to do that related to their age and ability and at the same time needed doing: washing the dishes, for example, involved a washer, a dryer, and several putters-away. Without any words being said, they grew up understanding teamwork. Several of them had large families of their own. When we all attended Mom and Dad's golden wedding party, held in a large hall with different floor levels and other potential obstacles for young children, Leo and I noticed how teamwork was working in the third generation, too. Our nieces and nephews were unobtrusively keeping an eye out for each other's children. When Mom died very recently, Leo was 12,000 miles away here in England but the family kept in touch over the phone. As I heard different siblings and their adult children describing the celebration of her life on the phone the evening of her funeral, many of them talked about "the team": everyone had contributed photographs (more than 150 were collected to form a record of different parts of Mom's life); during the service, the siblings had each said a short piece, and Leo's was edited by one niece and read out by a brother; a niece had organized a CD recording to be made of the tributes, so everyone could have a copy; another was making a wonderful pudding—appropriately called "Ambrosia"—for everyone at the party; and everyone came to the phone to make sure Leo was included even though he was so far away.

CHAPTER **19**

Spotting Opportunities

If you are going to tip the implacable world in business or in private life you have first to spot the opportunity. You have to catch the moment, see the niche, register how the pattern is building or changing—and PUSH. The leverage you need is not about power, it's about applying just enough impetus in the right place and at the right time. Moreover, while people often assume that spotting an opportunity is about seeking potential benefits, it's also about avoiding risk, correcting errors and making things good again.

KEEPING ALERT FOR OPPORTUNITIES

Opportunities offer themselves to us every day if we only keep alert for them. There are chances to develop potential trends, alliances and niches in business, to build, deepen, improve or otherwise alter the significance of relationships, and to take small actions that help build toward fitness and well-being or help prevent its falling-off. All these ask of you (and sometimes this feels like a big "ask"!) is alertness—not the driven alertness of alarm, vigilance, excitement or ambition but an open-minded responsiveness to incoming sensory information and a mental preparedness to consider its implications.

Three meta-programs are fundamental to this: similar–different, away-from–toward and in-time–through-time.

1. SIMILAR–DIFFERENT: RECOGNIZING THE PATTERNS AND RECEIVING THE SIGNALS

Horses have what the NLP developer, trainer and consultant Robert Dilts calls "skin-sensitivity," and the way that they manage their world is therefore "skin-driven." Deering, Dilts and Russell translate this into business survival terms in their book *Alpha Leadership*:

> But if companies operating in volatile environments should not be guided by strategy, what should they be guided by? Our answer is that their "skin" should guide them: by the signals, weak and strong, that market-facing staff are constantly receiving. Actions should emerge from market contact directly, without rerouting through the center.
>
> *Alpha Leadership*, p. 23

Let's go back to the horse. Its skin is sensitive enough to register a fly landing on its body, as soon as, and exactly where, it lands. Something has changed—the fly is a signal of difference. The horse will automatically twitch to shrug it away. This is literally a skin-driven response. In a human context, Dilts would call this "responding to a weak signal" (see box).

Weak signals

"Anticipation starts with detecting weak signals. Everyone can hear a shout, but only those with exceptional sensory systems can hear the barely audible whispers where most of the opportunities and timely warnings lie." (Dilts)

Human beings often wait for a second, third or even subsequent signal before they act—and in so doing they lose immediacy and may miss opportunities. The horse reacts to the first indicator of difference (the new incoming signal). This may be appropriate, as in the case of the fly, but immediate responding can also get them into trouble. There are times when wise, or more experienced, horses realize that it's better to wait and see what happens next, as one of ours did when he slipped and fell down while being driven in a trailer. Rather than trying to get to his feet, he lay patiently where he was until we were able to stop and rescue him. He waited to see if the first information (falling) was going to be followed by further signals of danger. As it wasn't, he remained still, calm and unhurt.

Notice the very first signal

You can take a first signal of difference as an alert. To understand its implications and ensure you act appropriately, you can usually afford to wait for further signals. Reinforcing or confirming ones will tell you there's a pattern or a trend at work (similar); absence of further signals often (though not always) means that the first one can be ignored. More confirming signals still, and you definitely need to get the message!

In organizational or business terms, it really pays to develop skin awareness. Just as real skin gets less sensitive when it's covered up, so organizational leaders can become insulated by the hierarchies they manage until their skin awareness is deadened. Dilts and his colleagues said, "The successful companies of the future will be those with the best skin-driven planning systems, not those with the best plans." With thought and commitment, it's possible to build information-gathering and reporting structures that even in the largest companies allow information from the skin (in other words, the customers and front-line staff) to feed back rapidly to leaders and managers so that they can make the spot-on (fly and horse again!) decisions needed to keep the company competitive or even ahead of the field.

Using your similar–difference filter flexibly can help alert you to trends that are about to peak, as the trend forecaster Faith Popcorn wrote in 1991 in *The Popcorn Report*: "Just before consumers stop doing something, they do it with a vengeance."

To check whether more of the same now means that more of the same will continue, you need additional information to confirm or contradict the trend you have spotted. On the difference end of the spectrum, noticing what's not present in a service or market context may show up a niche that you could fill with a service or product.

Your personal life

In more domestic contexts, sensitivity to body language, voice tone and language use (especially phrases and metaphors that repeat) can give vital similar-based information that lets you know how others are feeling, not just how they are responding. Difference-based information, such as what might have been said or done but which hasn't been, or changes in expected or normal behavior and times when a conversation or a relationship suddenly goes off-track, can all alert you to ask yourself, "What changed? And how can I best respond?"

In relationships, receiving the weak signal of disappointment, frustration, distress, interest or attraction gives you the chance to test and, if appropriate, take action on what you have registered. "Was that a signal of something that needs fixing or repairing?" (Best do it now before it gets worse.) Or, perhaps, of a readiness to take the relationship further or change its emphasis? Throwing out a subtle hint that you have heard the possible message and are ready to respond may help you repair a breach while it's still reparable, or alternatively confirm your own interest in taking things further.

Health is another arena where monitoring similar and different can be important, and where the ability to notice weak signals can give you the opportunity of making corrections that can restore the status quo, be life-enhancing, or occasionally even life-saving. Nowadays doctors encourage their patients to become more self-aware, because illness prevention is better and more cost-effective than treating illness, in both individual and social terms. If you train yourself to notice small deviations from your usual baseline of functioning, you're more likely to spot possible indicators of something beginning to go wrong. Subsequent signals will then serve to confirm or contradict what you have noticed. Equally, noticing unexpected improvements in well-being or function can allow you to make what seemed good even better: for example, a client who already thought herself in good health started eating Marmite occasionally, and after a while found she was more energetic and alert. She decided to test her theory by discontinuing Marmite again, and after a few weeks found she felt less energetic again. She had been slightly deficient in the B vitamins without realizing it. Forming a theory and then testing it allowed her to turn an accidental improvement into a positive opportunity to enhance her health.

2. AWAY-FROM–TOWARD: MAKING THE RIGHT DECISIONS

It's often assumed that opportunity is a toward thing, all about grabbing something good. It's important, though, to understand that it's just as often about retreating when you need to or while you still can, about taking evasive action in good time and about rescuing things before they go pear-shaped—all are away-from situations. Sometimes you might turn down an opportunity in order to leave your time and energy free to take another—an example of going away-from in order to be able to go toward.

In his book *Toward a Psychology of Being*, the psychologist Abraham Maslow pointed out that human beings continually oscillate between two powerful motivations: safety (away-from) and growth (toward). When safety grows boring, we reach out toward the excitement of growth. When growth becomes dangerous, we head for safety again. This ongoing zigzag course operates in most people's lives, quite apart from their response to specific things they'd actually label as "opportunities."

3. IN-TIME–THROUGH-TIME: GRABBING OPPORTUNITIES AND SOLVING PROBLEMS

Without a sense of time past, time present and time future, we wouldn't be able to think in terms of opportunities, because we wouldn't have a way of relating our actions to our previous experiences or to our hopes and aims. Strongly in-time people may grab what feel like opportunities in the present, only to regret it later. A client of mine had a real eye for antiques but tended to sell them to the first potential buyer ("I need the money") rather than testing the market and waiting for greater opportunities at auction. Often, he later saw items he'd once owned come under the hammer, often realizing a far greater price. He had grabbed the opportunity as he saw it, but by doing so he missed a better one. Traders on the money markets make their living weighing up in-time offers against more through-time possibilities like these—and they don't always get it right either!

Through-time people, on the other hand, may take such a long view that their ability to act in the here and now is inhibited. A through-time view is important if you are to choose your course, but actually setting off can only happen as a result of actions in the present. Large-chunk–small-chunk flexibility can help you work out where to start and to appreciate how you can use things as small as a smile or as everyday as an e-mail as the leverage that begins something much bigger.

Milton Erickson, the therapist modeled so carefully by the early NLP developers, used a focusing technique to help his clients solve their problems by tapping into information which "they knew without knowing that they knew it." He would ask them to imagine a time in the future when their problem had been solved, and then ask what had happened in order for them to get there. The vast majority of clients knew exactly what had to happen, but the knowledge had been hidden even from them until they changed their perspective. Going through-time for just a few moments helped them find what was needed, and opened their eyes to the here-and-now opportunities to start changing things. You can do exactly the same.

Overall, there is no absolute criterion for "opportunity" other than how it seems to you at the time. Becoming more aware of how your meta-programming influences your ability to receive and act on weak signals from your external environment (in business and social life) and your internal one (your health and well-being) gives you more choices and more potential influence on your world.

WHAT OFTEN GOES WRONG

We can fail to spot opportunities and we can also spot them but fail to take them. Increasing your mental flexibility can help you become both a better spotter and a better taker.

Missing the weak signals

We can assume weak signals aren't enough basis for action, but just how different does different have to be in order for you to register it? Just how many drips in the same place does it take to tell you where the stone will eventually wear away? This is about encouraging yourself to honor any skin-based signal as evidence—of something—and then to ask what it's the evidence of. If you really need the signal to strengthen, you can always wait. Often, though, once you let the signal emerge into consciousness your gut response tells you that you unconsciously knew it anyway!

Missing the opportunity and giving up

Assuming that once you miss the first opportunity it's too late to do anything can be a mistake. The ultimate test of mental flexibility is readiness to turn around! The phrase "throwing good money after bad" describes the kind of mental—and often also emotional—inflexibility that makes you do more of the same thing only longer and louder in the hope that it will justify your original decision. Everyone can miss opportunities if their eye is off the ball: outstanding players may still retrieve that same ball by an athletic and accurate leap, but the rest of us can do well enough by paying more attention next time.

Assuming you aren't powerful enough to change things

Because we live in sequential time, everything follows something and precedes something else, so if you respond differently to a repeating pattern, however small, the difference you make will be changing the course of history—a plot line elaborated in many a sci-fi movie! This may be your small step that starts you off in a different direction, whether in business, in private life or on the path to better health. Such significant small steps can happen in the way you think, of course, not just in how you act.

Assuming you have to have a fully realized strategy before you act

Because of their very nature, opportunities can't be prepared for as such, although you can get yourself ready for them by developing a sense of where you would like to be heading and a sensitive "skin-awareness" for incoming information. Many people are inhibited from taking action on weak signals because they believe they have to have more information, or a fully developed strategy, if they are to follow through adequately. On the other hand, if you wait to be sure, someone else may have beaten you to the opportunity, or it may simply have disappeared because it was one that had to be grabbed now or never. This is the dilemma you face.

The solution is to change your understanding of what's involved, as Dilts and his colleagues explain. They point out in *Alpha Leadership* that the outstanding leaders (in both business and politics) hold firmly to their ultimate goals but are flexible in the way they respond to problems in achieving them. Although they put thought into strategies, they don't stick to them come what may: they adjust and adapt according to circumstances.

Heading for your chosen opportunity, you just need to bear in mind that signals of difference (problems or obstacles) can be taken as prompts to adapt, invent and approach your same goal along a different path. Spotting an opportunity is just the first step. Effective operators in business, personal relationships, health creation and maintenance aim themselves at the opportunities they have spotted and continue to monitor and correct their approach until they reach their goal. They understand that change and development are not things where you can tick the boxes and have done with it. For toward people that's the challenge and the excitement of growth. For away-from people, it's recognizing what's needed to maintain security and safety. For all of us, as my final chapter explains, managing ourselves successfully in the changing world around us is the biggest opportunity of all.

HOW THEY DID IT

Reinventing your approach until you succeed

Many years ago I had a client who had started his own business—and failed. He had had an interesting idea for a new product, which he endeavored to develop on his own. It was hard work, and he was not a natural salesman. When he first came to see me, he was bankrupt. But he was determined to get his idea into the marketplace, and really believed it could gain and hold people's attention. Facing every kind of failure, he thought flexibly. He sought, and found, a business partner with money to invest and a proven record in selling. They worked out a deal which allowed my client to continue developing his product and its varied spin-offs, while his partner organized production and promoted it. My client's faith in his invention was

➤

justified—it was a good product and the public took to it. Recognizing that he didn't have to do everything himself, and calling in someone with skills and experience better adapted to the marketplace was the key to a massive success and a way of life that suited him and his talents much better. Now the product has a world-wide reputation, as does my former client. Thanks to flexible thinking, he is able to continue doing what he does best, while his partner also does what he does best: the wheeling and dealing that keeps their venture afloat in a changing and challenging marketplace.

CHAPTER **20**

Making Decisions

In a sense, decision-making is what this whole book has been about. People often assume that the point about decision-making is whether you reach the right decision, and perhaps also whether you do that quickly enough. But actually, good decision-making is as much about the process as it is about the outcome. And the process often feels quite uncomfortable, just because it so often takes the form of an argument with yourself. Jonah Lehrer, author of the book *The Decisive Moment*, explains that one reason for this is that different parts of the brain are involved in processing different kinds of material, and therefore also in "making their bids" for particular kinds of outcomes. People know instinctively that this happens. How often have you heard someone say, "Part of me wants to do this, and part of me wants to do that"? The resulting discomfort can actually interfere with good decision-making. As Lehrer says, "The problem is that the urge to end the debate often leads to neglect of crucial pieces of information" (p. 191).

We don't have to be psychologists or researchers to manage such conflicts, or to reach good decisions. All we need is to cultivate our skin sensitivity (see Chapter 19), this time to register the thoughts and feelings that we receive internally, so that we can benefit from what they offer us: information. When I trained as a therapist, our trainers used to say: "Always reassure clients when they say they are confused, and tell them how valuable confusion is. It's only out of un-certainty that new growth and understanding can come." According to this, and to Lehrer's research, we may feel more comfortable being certain but we may also be dangerously blinkered!

Making the best of it

One of the enabling presuppositions of NLP is that people make the best decisions they can at the time, with the information available to them. In that sense, every decision is a "best" decision, relatively speaking. It's worth reminding yourself of this when you feel a past decision was the wrong one. Whatever happened as a result, you did the best you could at that time. Nonetheless, we can get better at decision-making.

WHY DO WE MAKE DECISIONS?

Decisions are things we make every day, sometimes with a lot of thought and sometimes with very little. Our decisions are based on a number of contrasting—and sometimes conflict-ing—things, such as careful evidence weighing, habit, intuition and impulse. What do these all have in common? The intention of serving our interests. This is another of the presuppositions that NLP has found it useful to make, and although some decisions can seem catastrophic or self-damaging, on the surface at least, it pays to probe for an underlying intent that is actually intended to be self-supporting, self-protecting or even self-enhancing.

One of my early clients had gotten into a pattern of wrecking his own life by spoiling every worthwhile relationship he had. He ditched his girlfriend, gave away his dog and was on the point of splitting up his work partnership. He could see there was a pattern operating, but not why, and he wanted it to stop. He couldn't believe that the pattern actually served a useful purpose, yet when we dug down that was exactly what it did. In his childhood, a series of good things had all come to an end through the decisions of others. Happiness there was, but every time he thought things were OK at last someone intervened in his life for their own good reasons, and his happiness ended. What he learned, as he told me, was that "all good things come to an end." That being so, the only power he felt he could have was to end them himself. His self-damaging adult behavior was the result: a perfectly logical, if quite unconscious, away-from strategy. But although he was right as a child when he recognized that a pattern was operating, he didn't then have enough information about adult motivation to draw the right conclusion, one which would have allowed him to trust good experiences that came to him as a result of his own choices and actions. There was important information he didn't have access to, so he couldn't take it into account.

GETTING THE RIGHT INFORMATION

While respecting the self-caring intent that underlies the decisions we arrive at, we can help ourselves get better at gathering and processing information before we make our choices.

- You can get better quality information, which means being alert to weak signals and being prepared to act on them, as I explained in the previous chapter. To do this, you need to develop your acuity in spotting patterns (sorting for similarities), registering breaks in patterns (sorting for differences) and noticing and reading body language.

- You can get information that is more comprehensive and more rounded by including other points of view (perceptual positions on page 138) rather than relying only, or largely, on your own.

- You can consider your possible options in the light of both in-time and through-time perspectives, creating a dynamic relationship, almost a conversation, between them. This helps you anticipate and evaluate possible consequences—both desirable and undesirable—so that you are more fully informed and prepared.

- You can learn to understand and estimate your own and other people's default meta-program preferences, studying to work with them rather than being caught up and possibly tripped up by them.

- Within your instinctive clustering of meta-program preferences, you can learn to trust your strengths—and thereby take pressure off your limitations—in helping you collect, evaluate and sort information relevantly and purposefully. And you can back this up by drawing on the supporting, contrasting or complementary strengths of others, so that your information base and your skill set are enhanced to make for better quality choice and decision-making.

THE KEY META-PROGRAMS

All meta-programs play a part in making choices, because they govern how you select the information you are working with. However, decision-making is particularly influenced by four meta-programs:

1. away-from–toward

2. association–dissociation

3. in-time–through-time

4. inner-directed–outer-directed

1. AWAY-FROM–TOWARD: WHAT FUELS YOUR DECISION?

Fuel is fuel, whichever direction it drives you. Some people have no difficulty in making decisions—in fact, they make them too easily! They respond positively to the implied "invitation" (pleasure) or to the implied "threat" (danger). Such immediate and primitive processing works fine where once-in-a-lifetime opportunities or life-threatening dangers are involved, but how often is that truly the case? A possible life partner is not going to be snatched up by someone else, like a bargain in the sales, if you don't make your mind up immediately. Emotional danger is rarely as fatal as physical danger, even though it can feel as alarming. As a way of managing life, following immediate impulses can set up all kinds of problems in the long term.

2. ASSOCIATION–DISSOCIATION: WHEN IS IT BEST TO ACT ON FEELINGS?

Any decision is only as good as the quality of the information on which it's based, and that includes whether you're tapping into logical- or feeling-based brain processing. The association–dissociation meta-program helps us manage the seesaw possibilities of emotional involvement and distance. We need to know what we like or fear but we don't have to act on feelings every time, however strongly they may suggest toward or away-from behavior. We need to know what makes logical sense, but sometimes acting according to sense alone ignores emotional or gut-level information that may turn out to be crucial. Better decisions are likely to happen if you make a habit of consulting both your left-brain logic and your right-brain "gut feeling" intuition.

3. IN-TIME–THROUGH-TIME: BEING IMPULSIVE OR PLANNING AHEAD?

People who are in-time can often be impulsive, and it may be that their decisions are more often influenced by the emotional part of their brain. Sometimes this hastiness results in unfortunate consequences longer term. Impulsiveness is one thing, and intuition is another. Although the message "Act now!" seems to be the same, there's actually an important difference between the kinds of processing involved. How can you tell the difference between a "want it now" impulse and a "that's it" message that comes from intuition? Intuitive information can "arrive" on your mental screen of awareness with as much force and as little "back-up" reasoning as the impulsiveness. How can you work out which is which?

The clue you need may be in the degree of emotion involved, or the amount of rationalizing you find yourself doing in support of your choice. On the whole, in-time impulse is strongly felt and we tend to rationalize decisions based on it after we've made them. Intuition also seems right to us, but the difference is that its messages are often strangely lacking in emotion. In my experience, intuition is the result of rapid mental processing at an unconscious level. It does have good supporting information to back it up, but this information only tends to appear on the screen of your consciousness later on, if at all. The reason it comes without emotional loading is that it comes from a different part of the brain, and one that has already evaluated the evidence! Learning to trust your intuition and separate its commands from those of feeling-driven impulse is part of developing a different kind of "skin-sensitivity": a sensitivity to different kinds of information from within yourself.

4. INNER-DIRECTED–OUTER-DIRECTED: WHO'S DRIVING YOUR BUS?

Quite often we find ourselves dithering, or even conflicted, about a decision because it actually or potentially involves a choice between doing what we want and doing what someone else wants or what our beliefs tell us we should. People whose operating base is toward either end of this meta-program are likely to act on their programming, but may sometimes regret it later. The people who experience such dilemmas most strongly tend to be those whose default settings on this spectrum are somewhere in between the extremes. Teasing out what's directing you or pulling your strings gives you a way to disentangle this. Sometimes it's enough just to ask yourself, "Says who?"

WHAT OFTEN GOES WRONG

Decision-making is not a science—nor indeed is it an art. We need to demystify it and think of it just as something that we do every day with regard to all kinds of issues. Like walking, each decision is a step. As with steps, decisions can add up to direction and to progress. What's important is how you do it and how you use each decision to confirm or correct the direction your life journey is taking. Each decision makes a difference, but usually it doesn't make all the difference! Remembering this can help you survive those moments when decision-making seems to have gone astray. Let's look at some of the more common problems that arise.

Allowing lots of little decisions to become unwanted habits

Eating too much, drinking too much, spending too much are all the result of hundreds—perhaps even thousands—of individual small-chunk decisions based on an in-time, toward and inner-directed constellation of meta-programs. And, of course, their effects can multiply. Provided someone wants to change, often they can simply reverse the pattern, one small decision at a time. Alcoholics Anonymous teaches its members and their families to think "one drink at a time" and to take "one day at a time," because chunking right down to a single yes/no decision every time you are tempted to have a drink (or eat something indulgent, or buy something that tickles your fancy) means you don't feel you're tackling a lengthy, large-chunk program of self-denial. The curious thing, of course, is that stacking up a great number of small, healthy choices does result in a large-chunk outcome: building a habit that leads to greater health.

A friend of ours was putting on weight, and made a series of decisions to not have a cookie at tea and coffee times. The no-cookie habit gradually resulted in natural weight loss. A client who enjoyed buying clothes learned to enjoy choosing clothes in catalogues instead. She discovered she could "choose" as many clothes as she liked, while only buying a few of them!

Finding it hard to reach a decision

66 It's not easy to make up your mind when your mind consists of so many competing parts. 99

JONAH LEHRER, *The Decisive Moment*, p. 201

Usually, indecision signals the need to process different kinds of information as well as information that is conflicting. Forcing yourself to make up your mind prematurely is not the answer. How can you weigh up things that have such different bases as emotion and reason or short- and long-term payoffs? What you need to consider first is what kinds of information you are trying to process and what each part of your brain is trying to achieve for you in pressing its case:

Pleasure now—problems long term?	Restraint now—opportunity lost forever?
Risk now—new directions and new rewards later?	Safety now—security and boredom long term?

To answer these questions, you have to be mindful of how your mind approaches things, teasing out the strengths and liabilities of its approach in order to make a decision that works for you as a whole.

WHEN YOU MAKE THE "WRONG" DECISION

It would be nice to feel confident that the decision you are about to make was going to be a right one. What you can be certain of, however, is that you can ensure it's the best you can make at this moment. Decisions that were made with the best intent, on the basis of the best information, can still be invalidated by events, including the decisions of other people.

The best follow-up to a decision that turns out to be "wrong" is to acknowledge its wrongness and then to backtrack. It's far worse to stick grimly with the decision just because you made it—or to force someone else to, just because they did. Facing a wrong decision is a time for picking yourself up, dusting yourself off and starting all over again—either updating your goals in the light of changed circumstances and new information or simply updating your strategy for achieving them.

WHEN YOU ACT ON UNEXAMINED ASSUMPTIONS

Often we make a decision to do or not do something on the basis of something we assume. Often, the assumption involves a hidden toward: for example, "They'll like me more if . . ." Or a hidden away-from: for example, "They won't approve if . . ." You may not even realize the assumption is there. It's a gap in your mental pavement that you've stepped over without realizing. If you are dithering about a decision, ask yourself what stops you. Usually, this will surface any negative assumptions you may be making. You can also ask yourself what you think will happen if you do make that decision—and what you expect if you don't. Questions like these help you dig deeper into the processing that's going on beneath the surface of your brain so you discover what's really blocking you. You will usually be surprised by how quickly an answer comes to your self-questioning, and how revealing it can be.

Every day you face an unremitting schedule of decisions, from opening your eyes to closing them again. In facing the challenges and opportunities of breakfast, work, home and leisure that require decisions for today and for the future, you are automatically equipped with the most comprehensive sorting equipment possible: your meta-programming brain. My work with colleagues and clients over the years has shown me that actual decisions matter far less than how people cope with what happens after they have made them. This is where your new understanding and more developed mental flexibility are at your service. The decisions you make with these as your allies are some of your biggest, best and most exciting decisions of all.

CONCLUSION

Surviving and Thriving in a World of Change

We may feel we can't change the world, but in changing ourselves we change the impact we make in the world. And a ripple is created that's different from how it might otherwise have been . . .

What if you were to use your understanding of meta-programs, and your developing flexibility in managing them, as a tool not just for surviving in our changing world but for actually thriving in it? A tool to help you recognize your own unique way of making sense of things and to capitalize on it? A tool to help you accept and work around your inevitable and very human blinkeredness? A tool that could help you fathom the mysteries of other people, and navigate the hazards of families, teams and organizations with more confidence and more effectiveness? A tool that opens your eyes even wider to the exciting, playful, never-ending possibilities of engaging for real with the dynamic complexity of things?

At this time of rapid social, technological, political and ecological change we need all the tools we can get. The amazing thing is that this tool is already installed in your brain. I hope that reading this book has helped you recognize just how astonishing you already are—and how much more you can do now that you know this. In evolutionary terms change is something that continues. We can't stop it, we don't need even to try—because the more we know about the human brain, and the more flexible we become in working with its possibilities, the more we can ride the changes. Better than that, in shaping ourselves we can actually shape *them*.

Bibliography

Allingham, Margery, *More Work for the Undertaker* (Heinemann 1949), Penguin edition (1963)

Claxton, Guy, *Hare Brain, Tortoise Mind*, Fourth Estate (1998)

Covey, Steven R., *The 7 Habits of Highly Effective People*, Simon & Schuster (1999 edition)

Deering, Anne, Robert Dilts and Julian Russell, *Alpha Leadership*, John Wiley (2002)

Dilts, Robert, *Modeling with NLP*, Meta Publications (1998)

Fisher, Roger, and William Ury, *Getting to Yes*, Penguin (1991)

Gallwey, Timothy, *The Inner Game of Tennis*, Pan (1986 edn)

Grinder, John, and Richard Bandler, *The Structure of Magic II*, Science and Behavior Books (1976)

Jenner, W. J. F., *The Tyranny of History*, Penguin (1992)

Lehrer, Jonah, *The Decisive Moment*, Canongate (2009)

Leon, Donna, *Willful Behavior*, Arrow (2003)

Popcorn, Faith, *The Popcorn Report*, Doubleday Currency (1991)

Pratchett, Terry, *Monstrous Regiment*, Doubleday (2003)

Rath, Tom, and Donald Clifton, *How Full Is Your Bucket*, Gallup Press (2004)

Sayers, Dorothy, "The Vindictive Story of the Footsteps That Ran" (1928), in *Lord Peter Views the Body*, New English Library (1974)

Senge, Peter M., *The Fifth Discipline*, Century Business (1990)

Soros, George, article in *New York Review of Books* (November 2008)

Spurgeon, Caroline, *Shakespeare's Imagery and What It Tells Us* (first published 1935), Cambridge University Press (1958 edition)

Toffler, Alvin, *Future Shock*, Pan (1974 edition)

Further Reading

All the books quoted in the text or listed in the Bibliography have intrigued or inspired me in one way or another. This is a very personal list of others that have helped my own stretching and strengthening. I hope you will enjoy exploring some of them too.

Books to help you explore NLP

Andreas, Connirae, and Steve Andreas, *Heart of the Mind*, Real People Press (1989)

Andreas, Steve, *Transforming Your Self*, Real People Press (2002)

Andreas, Steve, and Connirae Andreas, *Change Your Mind and Keep the Change*, Real People Press (1987)

Bandler, Richard, *Using Your Brain for a Change*, Real People Press (1985)

Bandler, Richard, and John Grinder, *Frogs into Princes*, Real People Press (1979)

Bandler, Richard, and John Grinder, *Trance-Formations*, Real People Press (1981)

Bandler, Richard, and John Grinder, *Reframing*, Real People Press (1982)

Cameron-Bandler, Leslie, David Gordon, and Michael Lebeau, *Know How*, Real People Press (1985)

Charvet, Shelle Rose, *Words That Change Minds*, Kendall-Hunt Publishing Co. (1995)

James, Tad, and Wyatt Woodsmall, *Time Line Therapy and the Basis of Personality*, Meta Publications (1988)

Strengths-based books

Buckingham, Marcus, *The One Thing You Need to Know*, Simon and Schuster (2005)

Buckingham, Marcus, and Curt Goffman, *First, Break All the Rules*, Free Press Business (2001)

Buckingham, Marcus, and Donald Clifton, *Now, Discover Your Strengths*, Free Press Business (2002)

Books about thinking differently

Argyris, Chris, *Teaching Smart People How to Learn*, Harvard Business Review Classics (2008)

Kline, Nancy, *Time to Think: Listening to Ignite the Human Mind*, Ward Lock (1999)

Laborde, Genie, *Influencing with Integrity*, Syntony Publishing (1984)

Rashid, Mark, *Life Lessons from a Ranch Horse*, David and Charles (2004)

Semler, Ricardo, *Maverick!*, Arrow (1993)

You might also like to explore some of my other books

Effective Communication in Practice, with Jan Pye, Churchill Livingstone (1998)

Brief NLP Therapy, with Ian McDermott, Sage (2001)

The NLP Coach, with Ian McDermott, Piatkus (2001)

Your Inner Coach, with Ian McDermott, Piatkus (2003)

The Coaching Bible, with Ian McDermott, Piatkus (2005)

Schooling Problems Solved with NLP, J. A. Allen (2001)

Solo Schooling, J. A. Allen (2003)

Score More for Dressage, J. A. Allen (2006)

What Horses Do for Us, J. A. Allen (2009)

Index

About the Author

Wendy Jago trained as a psychotherapist in the early 1980s, but first became interested in NLP when her course tutor suggested she read two recently published books by Richard Bandler and John Grinder: *Trance-formations* and *Frogs into Princes*. This began a period of learning about the subject, attending workshops and courses. Wendy soon began using NLP with her clients and in her training of other therapists. She qualified as a practitioner, master practitioner and finally as an NLP coach, and is now working with private individuals, groups, international corporations and public-sector organizations. She has co-written five books about NLP, as well as becoming the first person to apply it to the betterment of communication between riders and horses.

If you would like to inquire about coaching, contact Wendy at wendy@jagoconsulting.eclipse.co.uk.

If you enjoyed this book, visit

www.tarcherbooks.com

and sign up for Tarcher's e-newsletter to receive
special offers, giveaway promotions, and
information on hot upcoming releases.

TARCHER
PENGUIN

Great Lives Begin with Great Ideas

If you would like to place a bulk order
of this book, call 1-800-847-5515.